THE POETRY GAMES: TRUTH OR DARE?

SOUTH LONDON

Edited By Sarah Washer

First published in Great Britain in 2018 by:

Young Writers
Remus House
Coltsfoot Drive
Peterborough
PE2 9BF
Telephone: 01733 890066
Website: www.youngwriters.co.uk

All Rights Reserved
Book Design by Ben Reeves
© Copyright Contributors 2017
SB ISBN 9781-78896-039-7
Printed and bound in the UK by BookPrintingUK
Website: www.bookprintinguk.com
YB0343U

FOREWORD

Welcome to *The Poetry Games: Truth Or Dare? - South London.*

For this Young Writers poetry competition we encouraged self-expression from secondary school pupils through a truth or dare format. The 'truth' entries reveal what it's like to be the writer, what they are passionate about; be a sincere expression of the poet's emotions or share their hopes, dreams and ambitions. The 'dare' entries are provocative enough to question the conventional and voice the writer's opinion; they may fight for their beliefs in verse or just tell a poetic tale of an audacious adventure.

We encouraged the writers to think about the technical aspects of their poems' compositions, whether they be an acrostic, haiku, free verse or another form. We also asked the young poets to consider the techniques they employ within the poem such as metaphors, onomatopoeia, rhyme and imagery.

I'm so impressed with both the content and the style of the poems we received and I hope you enjoy them as much as I have. I'd like to congratulate all the writers who entered this competition and took up the challenge to join Team Truth or Team Dare.

Enjoy!
Sarah Washer

CONTENTS

Independent Entries

Jessica Frank (11) — 1

Ark Putney Academy, Wandsworth

Alexandre Gallimore (13) — 2
Tyrese Fearon (14) — 4
Chakiena Shannon Dawson (13) — 6
Alicia Grilli (12) — 8
Alisha Noor Hissoob (13) — 9
Phoebe Munday (12) — 10
Afia Rehman (12) — 11
Tianna Tashauna Willis (12) — 12
Germany Pattanavichate (13) — 13
Amelia Tugwell (13) — 14
Nicol Ramos Nardello (14) — 15
Elena Cristina Simon (12) — 16
Kinza Baig (12) — 17
Rochelle Smith (14) — 18
Mia Tickel (13) — 19

Eltham College, London

Alexander Golshan-Ebrahimi (12) — 20

More House School, Chelsea

Leen Altanger (13) — 22
Jemima Rhys Jones (12) — 24
Yesim Brunini (12) — 25
Clara Hughes (12) — 26
Elena Sanz-Paris (12) — 28
Anastasie Eckert (12) — 29
Ella Eastwood (12) — 30

Putney High School, London

Honor Appleby-Taylor (12) — 31
Abi Hession (14) — 32
Sirena Waas (11) — 34
Isabella Chiarotti (13) — 36
Penny Hampden-Tuner (12) — 38
Ines Farah — 40
Tierney Dennis — 42
Bella Conroy (14) — 44
Eleonora Gallenzi (14) — 46
Zahra Ahmad — 48
Natasha Murrin — 49
Lara Gilodi-Johnson — 50
Naya Nwokorie — 52
Sophie Williams (14) — 53

Sydenham School, Sydenham

Fartun Hussein Ali (11) — 54
Asma Bashira Toure-Mathys (12) — 56
Sophie Kiondo (11) — 58
Sakinah Hasani (11) — 60
Charlotte Allsopp (12) — 62
Rihanna Bangura (11) — 64
Anna Smith Kirchner (11) — 66
Ameenah Arewa (11) — 68
Isla MacPhee (12) — 70
Evie Fraser Alderson (11) — 72
Nicole Kosiorek (11) — 74
Chiamaka Onumonu (11) — 76
Martha Simons (12) — 78
Samiat Blessing Adediran (12) — 80
Rasika Elangeswaran (11) — 82
Nyobi Bassey (11) — 84
Holly Yvonne Mary Whittington (12) — 86

Maisie Newman (11)	88
Emily Grace Joanna Slanickova (11)	90
Nell Rosie Wolstenholme (12)	92
Hayat Abdi (11)	93
Monifa Onitolo (11)	94
Jessica Mae Green (12)	96
Kathryn Alice Hart (11)	98
Hannah Oakey Adams (11)	100
Alexandra Iwaniuk (11)	102
Ruby-Mae Kelly (12)	104
Cara May Mulligan (11)	105
Dita Montgomery Kellett (11)	106
Alena Hoangova (12)	108
Kaiya Beaton (12)	110
Caitlin Clarkson (11)	112
Eleanor Chambers (11)	114
Beatrice Rutherford (11)	116
Isabella Mensah (11)	118
Nina Funa Visser (11)	120
Sylvia Sheppard (11)	121
Anya Nwakaego Umeh (11)	122
Ayodele Afful (12)	124
Mauve Emerald Roslynd Mawston (11)	126
Mika Eilon (11)	127
Maryam Bah (11)	128
Isabella Caseley (11)	130
Rumaysah Z Saeed (11)	132
Ruby Bremner (11)	134
Ella Sinnott-Behrmann (11)	136
Maya Reuben (11)	137
Sharia Cherryanne Pascal (11)	138
Emma Winter (11)	140
Fawzia Ali (11)	141
Lauren George-Wood (11)	142
Heidi Elizabeth Leon Quezada (12)	144
Maariya Maya Alom (11)	145
Aaisho Buule (11)	146
Sophia George-Pendleton (12)	147
Savannah Wood (11)	148
Emily Barker (11)	149
Iris Kemp (11)	150
Jessica Ansbro (11)	151
Lola Capstick (11)	152
Xia Lin (11)	153
Lillian Terletska (11)	154
Tiana Foster (11)	155
Izzi Phillips (11)	156
Ellie-Mae Hogan (11)	157
Olivia-Jean Imaga (11)	158
Leela West (11)	159
Dotty Burdett (12)	160
Roberta White (11)	161
Tia George-Flavius (11)	162
Beatrice Lily Seaton (11)	163
Amy-Rose Louisa Masic (12)	164
Faith Esther Grace (11)	165
Abbigail Grima (11)	166
Halia Bakare (11)	167
Vishranthie Prapakaran (11)	168
Kirsty Louise Barnes (11)	169
Olivia Juutilainen (11)	170
Libby Alcock (11)	171
Eva Harris (11)	172
Kira Spencer Brown (11)	173
Jennifer Nguyen (11)	174
Naomi Walters-Collett (11)	175
Isabella Jones (11)	176
Fienna Isabella Santos De Jesus (12)	177
Sahar Azimi (11)	178
Victoria Odaranile (11)	179
Michaela Dadzie (11)	180
Francesca Vass Redford (11)	181
Zahra Mughal (11)	182
Edie Kelly (11)	183
Ashley Lefante (12)	184
Anna Williams (11)	185
Greta Kelly (11)	186
Layla Molina-Tittle (11)	187
Edith Sargeant (11)	188
Poppie Lola Sweetman (11)	189
Isla Steven (11)	190
Saffron Salsone (11)	191
Brooke Miller (12)	192

Callie Boydell-Loftus (11)	193
Poppy Mona Frayne-Cradick (12)	194
Theodora Carneiro E Silva (11)	195
Raphaelle Aklama (12)	196
Shathana Satkunaseelan (11)	197
Torree Henry (11)	198
Allegra McAuliffe (11)	199
Josie Gerard Hughes (11)	200
Vivien Uong (11)	201
Sydney Austin (11)	202
Tiana Christina Williams (11)	203
Grace Howlett (11)	204
Rihanna Harvey (11)	205
Rukhiaya Mahmood (12)	206

Thomas Tallis School, Blackheath

Jacky Li (14)	207
Freddie J H C Fullerton (13)	208
Susie Duckworth (11)	210
Lily Ijoma (12)	211
Lewis Atkins (13)	212

SCARS IN MY HEART

Dare

With a skip in my step, I marched to the door,
'Please sign up here to fight in the war,'
Feeling brave and patriotic whilst standing in line,
We felt like we were needed for the very first time.

After months of training, we knew we were prepared,
We were ready for battle but we were a little scared.
March, march, march, the rhythm on the stone,
The war will be swift, we'll soon be home.

Bang! Another dear friend collapsed in the sand,
Fear was gripping me - I could not stand.
Explosions all around me - I struggle to breathe,
My heart is screaming, I cannot leave.

A tenth of my troop made it back,
Clickety-clack, the train on the track.
The stitches and bandages will soon be gone,
But the scars in my heart will never move on.

Jessica Frank (11)

UNTITLED

Truth

I'm done with the diss tracks, done with the hate
If I have a problem I sort it out face-to-face
I don't care about your race
I ain't gonna discriminate no matter what you say
'Cause you want a reaction, you want a reply
Cussing my mum just so you can see me cry
Then we have a guy who tries to cause a fight
Then another who likes a girl but he's too shy
It's got to the point where I wanna die
Too fast, so many things happening in my life
Friendships broken, I try to make it right
By trying not to lie, by trying to say hi
I should give up, they're just using me like a toy
Bullying, yeah that's another point
Threatening for votes, hoping you would pick them
People who are bullying can also be a victim
Trying to slice, praying and hoping each day and each night
Texting every morning, I say you are my light
They're using guns and knives, taking lunch money, you think that's nice?
Not at all, I won't have it, unacceptable
Multicultural school, we should respect them all
I'm a lover, not a fighter, I'm smoke and you're a lighter
'Cause you're shining so much brighter when you and I elevate higher

They say...
This is a message, there's no more finessing
I call it a blessing, when we all stay resting
I love a girl, we're moving like mobility
Let's get together and spread positivity.

Alexandre Gallimore (13)
Ark Putney Academy, Wandsworth

SLEEP

Truth

Sleep is love,
Sleep is life,
Sleep is something you want,
When you want to feel all nice.
But sometimes we can't get sleep,
For reasons unknown,
When all you want to do is fall asleep,
So you can rest your bones.

To a bed I must go,
Where I can be all alone,
No one to bother me,
All of life shortly postponed.

Away from life's struggles
In a region I control,
No longer muddled,
In a good place I own.
No stress about problems,
So they can never blossom,
When I'm asleep I feel protected,
From life's objections.

Life does me dirty,
But yet it still expects me to show courtesy.
Life isn't worthy
Of those who know their journey.

To a bed I must go,
Where I can be all alone,
No one to bother me,
All of life shortly postponed.

However, sleep ain't all good,
Even though I wish it could.
Sleep consumes time
And keeps you all confined
From the people you actually like
The ones you like enough to waste your time.
But to others I don't mind
I don't think that is a crime.

To a bed I must go,
Where I can be all alone,
No one to bother me,
All of life shortly postponed.

Tyrese Fearon (14)
Ark Putney Academy, Wandsworth

Truth

Your words do hurt and make me sad
What did I do to make you hate me so bad?
I used to leave school with a grin on my face
I now leave school as a disgrace
I come home and my mum asks me, 'What's wrong?'
I just pray and pray that all of this could be gone.

I go to school and your words will ring in my ears
I run home with great big tears
I go straight to my room and close the door
And find something sharp to make me sore
I cry and cry because of the pain you caused
I go into school and people stare or take a pause
They used to ask me 'What is the matter?'
They used to laugh at me or walk away or even call me names
I used to wish that I didn't exist.

I pray and pray that I could just die
I then go to the tall bridge and start to cry
I stand on top of the edge
I then stumble and slip
I lose my grip
I scream so loud that I close my eyes

I see the white light shining bright
Now that I am gone, I hope you are impressed with what you do best
Now that I'm away, I hope you are ashamed
I know this sounds silly but I wasn't the bully.

Chakiena Shannon Dawson (13)
Ark Putney Academy, Wandsworth

WHY ?

Dare

W hat goes through your mind at night?
Are you really that desperate that you have to fight?
Do you have to hate?
You have sealed your fate.
Why are you so cold?
Your social media is bold, but not in a good way
Because of what you do, you will pay.
Am I wrong or just mad?
Whichever one, you are just bad.

H ow to we save society from negativity?
To make the world full of positivity?
Maybe spread a message: we are all equal, so
Don't be cruel by using social media.
Don't be mean when all you want to be is a normal human being!

Y ou ruined my life along with so many others.
We used to be so blue,
But you cause pain, hatred and sorrow.
You can change, just say stop.
Don't hide behind your accounts.
Something may be going on,
Fix up and make a change.

Alicia Grilli (12)
Ark Putney Academy, Wandsworth

CYBERBULLYING

Dare

S aying all of these things doesn't make you popular
What does is what you do to fix it
Because in the end you're going to be the one who begs
So it's better to just commit

T o all of the bullies out there
What the hell are you thinking?
You're going to become your worst nightmare
So how would it feel to be the one who's shrinking?

O bviously, you have something to say
Because if you don't, well that's strange
You're the one who's going to have to pay
So I suggest something has got to change

P lease, everyone, this needs to stop
You're just making the world turn
Because you're just going to turn into a big, fat flop
But the truth is they shouldn't be the one to feel it
You should be the one to feel the burn.

Alisha Noor Hissoob (13)
Ark Putney Academy, Wandsworth

WHY?

Dare

Why do you put me down?
You call me names, you tell me I'm not worthy,
I don't deserve to live this way, I'm human, you're human,
We are the same, so why?
Why do you think this is going to take you somewhere?
Words do hurt, make me feel sad when I haven't done anything bad.
You may think I'm hurting inside, but why?
Do you think I'm going to hide?
You're just a bully, nothing but a coward, who's jealous of people like me.
Am I really as bad as you make me feel,
Or the person who you want me to be?
I might not have loads of friends like you,
But together, me and my friends are stronger,
You will never break us,
I really don't hate you, it's just a pity that you are fake.
So one question that needs to be answered is...
Why?

Phoebe Munday (12)
Ark Putney Academy, Wandsworth

WAR!

Dare

What does war bring?
Revenge, happiness or sorrow?
It's a sad 'popping ad' that comes into your brain with a ding,
You can't get rid of it, nor can you escape it.
It's trapped onto your fingers like a desolated ring,
But more painful!

Who killed those vulnerable children - war or people?
It creates hatred.
Unconsciousness lingers around in your brain,
Especially for the hearts who have no room for war.

War is not created by the bombs or guns,
But created by you and placed into your hearts.
Stop striking people with the chilling knives!
Don't make the Earth a bomb!
Because the only thing you've bombed is your home!

Afia Rehman (12)
Ark Putney Academy, Wandsworth

VICTIM VS BULLY

Dare

Sticks and stones may break her bones,
But words can also hurt her.
Compared to that manipulator, she is a right disaster.
He thinks of himself as a lion, but really he's just jealous,
She's trapped in the bubble of peer pressure,
She dares him to share her pain.

Sticks and stones won't break her bones,
But words will not take over.
Her height is fine, her personality is kind
And it will be respected.
She has a mouth,
She's a lion inside.
She's popped the bubble of peer pressure,
She dares him to not be the bully he once was
And all will be forgotten.

Tianna Tashauna Willis (12)
Ark Putney Academy, Wandsworth

'FOR ALL I GIVE'

Dare

For all I give
I never take
I'm held captive
By the choices I make.

I care too much
For the world
It is a clam
But I see the pearls.

You push me back
To the start again
Now I'm in pitch-black
Cos where we started it was pain.

I'm pushed and shoved
Even if I give my love
The labels you give me
Fit like a glove.

Should I give up or give in
Either way I'll never win
All your words are as sharp as a pin
Whatever you do you'll never let me in.

Germany Pattanavichate (13)
Ark Putney Academy, Wandsworth

WAR!

Dare

Bang - man down
Bang - another dead
We always want to frown
When we see the blood on their heads
We are all human
We are all the same
So, if you kill a man
What pride do you gain?
These wars that go on
What are they for?
They always go wrong
So why start more?
The people around us
They all feel shame
But why should we feel cursed by our skin?
There's no one to blame
The wars that are happening
When are they done?
When this war is over
Will it be the last one?

Amelia Tugwell (13)
Ark Putney Academy, Wandsworth

HIDDEN...

Dare

She once stood where I stood,
Once laughed how I laugh,
Dreamed like I dream.

But a part of her hid,
Nobody knew what was going on.

A mother,
A sister,
An aunt.

Laughter had turned into tears,
A dream had died.

Her son alone,
Overwhelmed,
Unable to react to the fact she wasn't there.

Her sister, mother and father,
Collapsing on each other,
Speechless that she was gone.

Nicol Ramos Nardello (14)
Ark Putney Academy, Wandsworth

WORLD'S END

Dare

Tomorrow might not come,
The world is at its end.
There are no birds tweeting,
The last text was sent.

The last bird flew,
The last music played.
The last thing was glued,
The last food was made.

The last couple kissed,
The last glasses clinked.
The last thing was heard
And that's about it.

The day the world ends,
Cherish the moments.
The day the world ends,
Your life is over.

Elena Cristina Simon (12)
Ark Putney Academy, Wandsworth

EQUALITY

Truth

We must bring racism to an end,
This is a message I must send.
We are all cruel,
Is this a rule?

We must all stop,
No one is at the top.
We still have some time,
To put an end to our crime.

We all feel,
We all heal.
We go through pain,
Just to gain.

We all have the ability
To create.

Kinza Baig (12)
Ark Putney Academy, Wandsworth

WHY BULLY?

Dare

Bullying,
Why do it,
Why hurt me?

Bullying,
Words can hurt.
I am not sure why,
But all I seem to know is,
It makes me cry.

Bullying,
It gets to me,
But when will they see,
Their cruel words are hurting me?
Help me.

Bullying,
Please stop,
Just stop,
Help me.

Rochelle Smith (14)
Ark Putney Academy, Wandsworth

BULLYING

Dare

You are the bully who says I'm fat
I am the victim who is bored of that
You are the bully that ruins my day
I am the victim and that's not okay
You are the bully who gets in my head
I am the victim, you make me wish I was dead
You are the bully who gets under my skin
I am the victim and I'm going to win!

Mia Tickel (13)
Ark Putney Academy, Wandsworth

POEM ON TRUTH

Truth

I feel so derelict inside,
Someone's life, no other than a lie.
All night, as I cry,
I remember their bye-bye.

I cannot tell you how much,
The pain kills me, like a dagger in my heart.
It plays the part exceedingly well,
You won't understand, until you hear the bell.

It wakes you up, at the middle of the night
Or maybe in the morning, when you find your first fright.
Horror can't replace the sadness that you feel,
The correct words to use are 'like a never-ending wheel'.

I cannot laugh, I cannot talk,
I can't even eat, using a fork.
Time can't bring the good in death,
And all night long, I stayed in bed.

Age is time's beggar,
And lots of time equals mega.
I will always treasure the breeze which I felt,
And never allow those memories to melt.

Always appreciate the things they do,
Because when they're gone, you have no crew.
I wish, I pray, all in one day,
Until I find out, there's a debt I have got to pay.

And I am speechless, because there is nothing to say,
Apart from the tears, that come down my way.

Alexander Golshan-Ebrahimi (12)
Eltham College, London

FREEDOM

Dare

Some try to control you, try to snatch away any freedom you may have,
What they don't realise is that freedom comes from within.
If you don't let them take away your laughter,
Your voice,
Your strengths,
Then you've won.

We possess more power than we know.

If you can make a charming song with those around you,
Then you've won.
Laughter and smiles.
You can still smile at those around you.
You can still offer peace and tranquillity.

We possess more power than we know.

If you still dust yourself off after stumbling to your feet,
Then you've won.
Show people that you only give in to what you want.
Who knows, you may just influence your friend to chase her dreams,
Not watch them drift away.

We possess more power than we know.

If you shoot the arrow, aiming for your felicity,
Then you've won.
We are all pressured to stay within boundaries,
Expected to submit to rules.
You don't have to insert yourself into life-risking situations,
But if you allow anyone to take away your laughter and smile,
Then you've died a long time ago.

We possess more power than we know.

Leen Altanger (13)
More House School, Chelsea

FREEDOM

Dare

Freedom is like a bird, flying in the night sky.
Freedom is feeling the wind in your hair.
Freedom is living, breathing, running.
Freedom can be anything; independence, trust.
Freedom is when you leave the nest, when you put yourself out there.
Freedom is relationships, democracy, fighting for your country.
Soon I hope that everyone will have a chance of freedom.

Freedom is like the sun and the moon.
Freedom is living each day like it's your last.
Freedom is where the sky is the limit.
Freedom is like a wild animal that cannot be tamed.
Freedom is when you are free to roam and roar.
Freedom is peace, love and loyalty.
Soon I hope that everyone will have a chance of freedom.

Freedom is light, laughter and loving.
Freedom is bliss, beauty, boldness.
Freedom is hope, happiness, joy.
Freedom is effortless and exciting.
Soon I hope that everyone will have a chance of freedom.

Jemima Rhys Jones (12)
More House School, Chelsea

FREEDOM

Dare

Freedom is a fresh new start!
For some people it might mean living a new life.

Freedom can also mean to live without fear,
To choose my own friends,
To make my own choices,
To do what I want,
To just be me.

Freedom is like a dog without a leash,
To wake up with no alarm clock,
To be free of any pain inside of me!

Freedom is fighting for what you believe in,
It doesn't matter what colour your skin is,
Freedom doesn't discriminate and has no limits.

I know this poem doesn't rhyme,
But freedom is just a matter of time!

Yesim Brunini (12)
More House School, Chelsea

FREEDOM

Truth

Freedom climbs high,
Like water free to flow,
A paradise in the sky,
An underwater glow.

Freedom comes with a cost,
Like a painful lie coated in an elegant truth,
Others will wander, lost,
Bent into the big, deep blue.

Freedom is not perfection,
Not trapped like a bird with no wings,
Perfection is code for imperfection,
Fill your lungs and sing.

Freedom is to spend a night in infinity,
Where you can live like each day is your last,
Where there are no limits to the mountains of liberty,
And no such meanings as 'outcast'.

Freedom feels like you can fly,
Like you are a bird soaring above the branches of hope,
Do not be afraid to try,
No more hanging on the ends of a rope.

Freedom is choices,
Where you can look beyond your fate,
You can find your voice,
And vouch against other people's hate.

Clara Hughes (12)
More House School, Chelsea

FREEDOM

Dare

What is freedom?
Nobody knows...
What do I think of freedom?
It is a feeling everybody owns.

If I were a bird,
I would fly myself,
Free from this place.
Over land and ocean,
To the end of the world.

If I were freedom,
I would be the colour green,
I would be the countryside.

But freedom isn't always good,
You don't always feel protected,
You can be murdered or stolen,
Nobody would know.

So, what do I think of freedom,
It is a feeling everybody knows.

Elena Sanz-Paris (12)
More House School, Chelsea

FREEDOM

Dare

If I were a bird I would fly far away
Away from the slavery,
Away from the manipulatives,
Away from all the unfairness of the world
And never come back.
That is when I will know I have freedom.

If I were the king of the world,
I would be a leader,
A leader of a great nation,
A leader of wise and free people.
I would not hide nor lie and stay where I belong,
Because now I truly know what freedom feels like.

Anastasie Eckert (12)
More House School, Chelsea

FREEDOM POEM

Dare

It's time to be free, let our minds fly
Don't know where I'm going as time passes by
Lift your head high and soar through the sky
Never look back, no saying goodbye
On our freedom we always greatly rely
So, stop picking sides or we might die
But don't say bye or we will cry
Never forget our time in the sky
Soaring above with freedom held high.

Ella Eastwood (12)
More House School, Chelsea

MOST DAYS

Dare

Most days I will wake up, not knowing what to think.
There is different news, unexpected shows of selfishness
You tell us it will be alright and somehow it is not.
I cannot trust your speeches, your little acts of slyness.

When we say 'politician', we think grand and strong
But I think weak and brittle and I know what you say is wrong.
Sometimes I trust the good, the ones who help us out
But there is always someone trying to encourage doubt.

You promise us things and we follow like sheep and a dog,
Then you trick us and don't live up to expectations.
We get hurt, we regret decisions,
We think it's our fault and it is truly yours.

And I find it easy to agree with you, when policies are right,
When you show us improvement and encouragement
But we realise that it can't be true, that no matter what
There is a liar, who will hide in disguise.

So I don't think you realise how much it scares us when you lie
To our faces, to the television, to the world.
When you look down on us as a group
Us as a person. Us as a world.

Honor Appleby-Taylor (12)
Putney High School, London

COLOUR ME GREY

Truth

I feel misunderstood
As though I'm frozen in time
But everything around me is still moving as the clock chimes
Their shades are growing brighter as mine starts to dim
They are draining my colour, letting darkness seep in

They think it's a contest
They think it's something to hide
A deadly secret we should all keep on the inside
They can act as though it's not real
They can wave it away
But it's something that I contend with every single day

If it's just a phase
If everybody feels the same
Why do we lock it in the basement as our pride burns in shame
The grey is pouring into me
My brightness is dim
The smile etched onto my face doesn't come from within

They say that they listen
But they only ever hear
They presume they understand me

That I have nothing to fear
That they have been where I'm standing
But right now I'm standing here

I'm hollow on the inside
Numb from within
I'm entirely grey now
On the outside and in
They are towering above me
In many vibrant hues
Some of them red, some are yellow and a few of them are blue

But as I am standing here, I have something to say
That each and every one of you has felt the same way
You've felt as though you're the only figure on the canvas the artist hasn't bothered to fill in
That every colour surrounds you, boxing you in

The thing is grey's a funny colour
A mix of black and white
It's just a splash of darkness
And it's full of light.

Abi Hession (14)
Putney High School, London

HELP ME UNDERSTAND

Dare

A fiery explosion on a train,
29 people injured. Tears flow.
Needlessly. Carelessly.
What have you achieved?

A suicide bomber at a concert,
23 lives lost. Hearts broken.
Viciously. Violently.
What have you achieved?

A massacre in a market,
12 dead. Fear unleashed.
Thoughtlessly. Brutally.
What have you achieved?

Mass shootings, suicide missions, hostages,
137 fatalities. Lives destroyed.
Evilly. Maliciously.
What have you achieved?

A truck through the crowds,
15 lives crushed. Infinite pain.
Mercilessly. Remorselessly.
What have you achieved?

These are the ones that are raw,
Countless others I refuse to recall;
Not because I want to forget,
But remembering will paralyse me,
Make me simmer and burn with hate.
Passionately. Madly.
What would that achieve?

And so I beg - please help me understand.
Is it in the name of Allah?
But He won't want this.
Is it in the name of your Islam?
But this is not the Islam we know.
Is it in the name of acceptance?
But we are one, my neighbour.

Why do you do this?
When will it stop?
Is it when all our tears are shed,
And life ends?

Sirena Waas (11)
Putney High School, London

WHAT HAPPENS

Truth

I told Her what happened,
How it happened,
When....
Everything.

So when the next day,
I arrive at the gates,
And see Her,
With some others.
I watch their heads flex closer,
Their hands shoot up,
To conceal Her mouth,
And hide Her silent shout.

The mute button is pressed.
I stand in the silence.
I watch Her turn to someone else,
I glimpse the different people,
Turning, facing to each other,
Their heads flexing closer,
Their hands shooting up,
Forming a sequence,
Like ants, scuttling, passing leaves in line.

When the volume gets turned up,
I am in the centre of a ring,
And become aware of figures turning,
Twisting,
Towards me.
As if I'm a leftover chip getting flung from seagull to seagull.
They interrogate me,
Ask me questions.
Their hands vigorously tapping and thumping my shoulders.
Then walk away.

The day after,
The same happens.
I am on my own.
I get stared at,
Laughed at,
And hushed murmurs spread like leaves catching the wind,
Flying, whipping around.

But it is my fault.
I told the truth,
And this is what happens.

Isabella Chiarotti (13)
Putney High School, London

WHY?

Truth

The slamming of the door echoes through the empty rooms
There are footsteps before she enters with her outside fumes

She sits every day and stares
In her flesh there are tears

Why would she do this?
This world is bliss

Like every day, it begins to rain
Enormous, liquid drops of pain

They dribble down, reflecting the moonlight
I wish I could say everything will be alright

But instead I simply miaow
She sees me now

I jump next to her and she calms
Like I'm a soothing balm

Her rough fingers comb my hair
And she whispers into the empty air

Then we fall asleep together
Like every day, forever and ever

She comes home again
She stares again

She cries, like always
I see her hurt in so many different ways

Why doesn't someone realise?
Someone must see the throbbing pain in her eyes

The days go by and the only difference is her ability to get up
I can see her determination burn up

Then one day the door opens
And with it a wave of unusual emotions.

Penny Hampden-Tuner (12)
Putney High School, London

BIG BOY

Truth

All bound up,
Everyone cramped up in the den
Of all different ages.
Two, five, seven or even ten.

Bright eyes shining
In the invisible darkness,
Trying to lift up
A dead weight.

Like a fishing net,
Going through the depths of the ocean
Capturing as many
Frantic fish as its merciless mouth can.

'No! I won't go! I won't!'
Says one tyke,
But only in his head,
Never out loud.

His parents smile down at him.
'You're going to school, Danny!
You're going to school like a proper big boy!'

Big boy. As if.
That's what we always
Dream about. Growing up.
Making our own declarations.

Caged. Trapped. That's
How we feel sometimes.
The unfairness of a childhood, is
Like being forced to do something
You will never like.

But we will speak out.
We will let our folks know
How we feel. And how we feel
About making our own choices.

All bound up,
Dreaming of the day
We will speak out
And make our own decisions.

Ines Farah
Putney High School, London

THE DIFFERENCE BETWEEN US

Dare

His skin is white,
Mine is black.
His eyes are blue,
Mine are green.
We may be different colours,
We may have different values,
But we shouldn't be treated differently.

The bus is busy,
He has a seat, I don't.
The colours are separated
as if we're the pieces on a chess board.
The white people win
Again,
But we shouldn't be treated differently.

I work harder than him?
He sits at a desk,
I clean.
He sips coffee,
I clean.
He shouts,
While I clean.

But we shouldn't be treated differently.

We may win or lose,
We may earn more or less,
We may look different - and the same,
But the difference between us shouldn't divide us,
We're more alike than you know.

We both breathe,
We both bleed,
We both grieve,
We are both human.
We shouldn't be treated differently.

Tierney Dennis
Putney High School, London

I'M REALLY ANGST OFF

Truth

The 'happy' that I appear to be,
Is a false image of the true me.
You say you know me well,
But you only know what I tell.

The real me is hidden,
Locked away,
Forgotten about,
Abandoned,
Because of you.

Constructive criticism you call it?
The truth by what measure?
You interpret me as the you, you hate.
These acidic jabs on my looks, opinions, intelligence, erode me.
You target my flaws, to hide your own.
I get that I am not perfect, perfect is impossible.

But these barbs are like food for you,
You crave it,
Like you're a heroin addict, you would hate to admit it.

The past me, the real me, I have become
And all that I have left is an echo
And the image you have built for me has stuck.

For wherever I go and whatever I do,
People will know me as the girl who was.

Bella Conroy (14)
Putney High School, London

I AM MAD

Truth

Don't think for a minute
That you know me,
Because I am madder
Than a star shooting through the sky.

I am madder
Than the smell of freshly cut grass -
And beyond that green expanse
Lies an uncharted maze of streets.

Yes, I am mad,
Mad as the wind.

Behind this whitewashed brick wall
There's an unbrainwashed fire;
Under the frozen pool
There is a beating drum
Thumping out a wild march,
Because I am mad,
Mad as a hurricane.

In the rivers of lava
That flow from my mouth,
In the streaming rays
That dart from my eyes,
Don't look for sense or peace,

Because I am mad,
Mad as a rolling stone.

Yes, I am mad,
Mad as a burning book.

Eleonora Gallenzi (14)
Putney High School, London

ANTI-SOCIAL MEDIA

Dare

Connecting the world or killing connection?
We're all desperate to show our perfection

We analyse our big friend lists,
While sitting alone, wondering why we're friendless

As insecurity creeps in, we need everyone's validation
Showing our best selves, giving into the idealisation

Measuring self-worth by numbers of comments
You become fixated on snapping photos, but it's nonsense

You're oblivious to the daily destruction hidden on your phone
As you're obsessed with earning the Instagram throne

We live in a world full of smart phones and dumb people,
Not realising our everyday lives are tainted by something lethal.

Zahra Ahmad
Putney High School, London

SAFETY CATCH OFF

Dare

The trigger clicks
Nothing can be done
The bullet leaves the chamber
Hope left for later
It hits like a wave
Pushing you back

Humans are strong
Though our hearts are weak
The heart stops beating
The lungs gasp for air
But there is no hope
Nothing is there

A word is a bullet
Mouth's a gun
Words can hurt us
Just look what they have done.

Natasha Murrin
Putney High School, London

THE LIGHTHOUSE

Truth

I stand alone
On this barren stretch of rock
Before lies the vast ocean.
Dark skies
One light
My light
Hits the only sign of life in hours.
Come to me
Keep me company
But not too close.

Oh, how I wish I could be somewhere
Surrounded by life.
Instead of me
The sky
The sea.
Happiness
Is just beyond my reach.

I was happy once.
A man and his wife
Lived within my walls.
A family.

Alas
The young couple passed
Their children moved away.

Lara Gilodi-Johnson
Putney High School, London

STARDUST

Truth

Stardust floats in a painful abyss
Light years long
Billions to come
The insignificance
Frightens
Intimidates
Stars are birthed
Billions
Stardust floats in eternal space
Sprawling in daunting beauty
Unknowing
And I crave significance
In this universe
Everything is
Too big
And life is too short
In comparison
To the stardust
Light years away.

Naya Nwokorie
Putney High School, London

MY EMPTY INSIDE

Truth

Some days I find it hard to look in the mirror
I convince myself nobody would miss me if I was gone
My scars tell stories I run away from
But my loneliness is trapped beside
Waiting for the day maybe someone will fill
The emptiness inside.

Sophie Williams (14)
Putney High School, London

THE FAULT IN OUR WORLD

Dare

Why do they do this?
Do they have to fulfil a destruction list?
If we go,
They *will* follow.
All these bad things they're doing to us,
Are they asking to be called scum?
Like smoking, it's bad for our air and your lungs,
When it's all over, people will say, 'Look what you've done!'
Watch when it all comes clashing
And you'll be rapidly falling,
Deeper and deeper,
Asking, 'Will it be over sooner?'
We've got to stop. Now! Today!
Before it's way too late.

Another thing that's terribly bad,
Every single one of those awful terrorist attacks,
Bombing these places,
Look at who has passed, every one of those innocent faces.
What did they do to you
To make you so angry that you had to do?
Watch when it all comes down
And you hit the ground.

Thud! You'll make a sound,
But no one's going to be around.

Everyone, we have got to stop this today,
Right now, before it's way too late.
Everyone, everybody, every shape, every shading;
The British, the Swedish,
Don't forget the Irish,
The Spanish, the Turkish and the Polish,
The Pakistanis, the Punjabis, also the Somalis,
Sri Lankan, Palestinian and Nigerian,
Austrian, Italian and Ethiopian,
Australian, Pennsylvanian and Romanian,
Jamaican, American and South Korean,
Chinese, Japanese and Taiwanese,
Vietnamese, Lebanese and Bhutanese,
Israeli, Iraqi and Yemeni,
Ugandan, Kenyan and Canadian,
Doesn't matter what you are:
Asian, European, Australasian, African or American,
You still have etiquette,
North, east, south or west,
The times we work together is when we're at our best.
The fault in our world stops now and the change starts today,
Not next month, not in two weeks, it starts this day.
Do you want tomorrow to be a better day?

Fartun Hussein Ali (11)
Sydenham School, Sydenham

THE LAST TIME

Truth

From the moment you hold your baby in your arms,
You will never be the same.
You might long for the person you were before,
When you had freedom and time
And nothing in particular to worry about.
You will know tiredness like you never knew it before
And days will run into days that are exactly the same,
Full of feeding and burping,
Whining and fighting,
Naps, or lack of naps.
It might seem like a never-ending cycle.

But there is a last time for everything.
There will come a time when you will feed your baby
For the very last time.
They will fall asleep on you after a very long day
And it will be the last time you ever hold your sleeping child.
One day you will carry them on your hip,
Then set them down
And never pick them up that way.
You will scrub their hair in the bath one night
And from that day on they will want to bath alone.
They will hold your hand to cross the road,
Never to reach for it again.

They will creep into your room at midnight for a cuddle,
Never to receive it again.
One afternoon you will sing and do all the actions,
But to never sing it again.
They will kiss you goodbye at the school gate.
The next day they will ask to walk to the gate on their own.
You will read a final bedtime story and wipe their last dirty face.
They will one day run to you with arms raised,
To never wake up to the joy.

You won't even know it's the last time,
Until there are no more times.
So while you are living the memories,
Preserve it.
Remember, there are only so many of them,
And when they are gone...

You will yearn for just one more day of them,
For one last time.

Asma Bashira Toure-Mathys (12)
Sydenham School, Sydenham

US?

Dare

Us? Us? Us?
What are we?
Are we lovers or haters?
Destroyers or creators?
Do we accept each other as family
Or ignore and abandon our loved ones?
Can we encourage one another to make a change
Or beat them down till there's no hope?
There's one of me and one of you
But together we make *us!*

Is it OK to call each other different
Even though we are brothers and sisters?
We are all the same, just choose to have a label
That gradually consumes our thoughts
And tells us this is what we are.
When we are more capable than we think we are
Will we live forever or will we be a never?
We are unique, not one person is normal.
Be you.
Just because you don't choose the same path as others
Doesn't mean you're not a star.
There's one of me and one of you
But together we make *us!*

You and me aren't so different at all.
I like blue but you might like pink.
I'm sometimes named a so-called tomboy
Whilst you're a beautiful queen.
Don't let anyone stop you dreaming.
Be you.
We could have been taught to be someone else
Than to learn to love ourselves and make our own way.
They might have taught us to like this type of person
When actually we like him or her.
Don't be a motionless, frightened mouse
Be more of a free-flowing, legendary lion.
There's one of me and one of you
But together
We make... *us!*

Sophie Kiondo (11)
Sydenham School, Sydenham

BULLIES

Dare

They think it's all fun and games
They laugh at her, call her names
Spit on her and pull her hair
She just wants somebody to care.
She cannot understand why
They push her down and make her cry
Is it because she's different
And they're all the same?
She lets the tears fall
And hides her head in shame
They see cuts on her arms
Call her a freak
And she's too scared to speak
To stand up for herself
She'd be standing alone
She wants to disappear
To just be gone.
The house is quiet but the pain is loud
She'll never be part of the popular crowd
And they will torment her day after day
So she leaves a note on her bedroom door…

Saying she's sorry
She can't do this any more
She's been thinking for a while

Had this carefully planned
A glass of water
Empty pill bottles crowding up her night stand
No one knew this pain ran so deep
When her only wish was just to go to sleep.

Ambulance and police lights flashing outside
Secrets uncovered
Things she tried to hide
Were brought to light.
As paramedics willed her to fight
They brought her back
Felt her breaking heart
And she knew this was when
The healing would start.

She won't be the same girl again.

Sakinah Hasani (11)
Sydenham School, Sydenham

START AND END

Dare

A clear, blue blanket surrounds the Earth,
It hides many secrets, more than we know,
Underneath, a vibrant carpet lays,
Containing uniquely shaped homes to many fish,
A rainbow on the soft sand, all different shapes and sizes,
Streamlined dolphins dive in and out of the turquoise water,
Titanic whales leap and splash around in the sea,
Causing waves instead of ripples,
This is the Great Barrier Reef before global warming.

Now, under the sea lies a ghostly, eerie and pallid carpet,
Bleaching and global warming have created a massive deathbed under the ocean,
What was once a vibrant, beautiful cloak over the sea bed,
Is now a sinister, pale sheet of random shapes,
The colourless corals are witches' claws, crooked and petrifying,
The wraith-like, pale spiders recoil and accept that their death is soon to come,
This is the Great Barrier Reef during global warming.

The rotten, dead corals look like fallen birds struck with rigor mortis,
A harsh layer of coffee-brown shapes take over the ocean floor,
These are miniature witches' arms,

Reaching out for the hope of life,
A huge graveyard of uncovered zombies,
The coral reef is burnt down and dead,
This is the Great Barrier Reef after global warming.

Charlotte Allsopp (12)
Sydenham School, Sydenham

THE WORLD AND ME

Dare

The world is a dark place
The clouds are grey
The animals are dying
People are turning against the world
It's desolate, it's dark
It's ugly
It's ashamed, it's sad
It's disgusting, it's angry
Once it had a smile on its face
Now a frown
Its friends; the moon, the sun
Didn't understand
Now it stands alone
In a corner of the universe
Watching the others play and laugh
It shivers, it stares
Time goes by
The other planets become no more
It still remains
It is still alone
It is still cold
Then a light surrounds it
It called it to come and play
They become friends

They cry together
They die together
Now the light stands alone
By itself, in the dark
Wishing the world was here
Now I tell this story on my deathbed
I remember when me and the world met
And how it was shy
I remember when we cried and smiled
I remember when it hugged me when I was scared
I remember this
How I slip through the universe's fingers
How it's warm and soft
I drift away to another land
Where me and the world will meet again
Maybe you'll see us dancing and playing
Laughing and crying
But *never* will you see us apart.

Rihanna Bangura (11)
Sydenham School, Sydenham

THREE VIEWS

Truth

Betty is my name
To others I am lame
As I walk through the gates
Terror awaits
Thud, thud, my heart pumps so fast
As I attempt to get to class
I feel so much dread
As I see her ahead
There is the bully

She smiles her evil grin
She bursts my happiness with a pin
I wait for the pain
But all she does is call me lame
I begin to relax
But then she hits me with the facts
I know it's all a lie
Yet I begin to cry
She is the bully

My name is Annie
And I may seem funny
But I am filled with regrets
And I'm trapped in many nets

I feel like I don't deserve life
If I could, I would use a knife
I am a bully

I turn myself in
I can't carry on being a pin
I listen to her speak
And I suddenly feel so weak
I want to leave and restart
Yet I can't leave and be like a cart
I must not cower from my wrongs
I must stand up tall and rewrite my songs
I was a bully

I can't reveal my name
I feel so much shame
I watched her cry
And I told so many lies
I backed her up
I feel as if I'm empty like a cup
One which holds every regret in the world
Because I helped a bully.

Anna Smith Kirchner (11)
Sydenham School, Sydenham

OUR EARTH

Dare

Look what we have done,
We have turned this world upside down,
This beautiful creation has turned into a big frown.
What about all the animals?
They have rights and feelings too,
But the humans don't seem to notice,
They don't have a clue.
People are chucking things in the ocean
Like it's some kind of bin
And people littering on the ground,
Making this world go dim.
This world is a wrecking ball.

Utopian to dystopian,
The world is a disaster.
Screaming, running,
It's all a big palaver.
Polar bears lying on their one cube of ice,
Is there a chance that they will survive?
Hurricane Irma,
Hurricane José,
The world is slowly ending,
Like the cycle of a rose.

As the world slowly falls apart,
The people carry on,
We need to try and fix this,
Don't they realise they are doing wrong?
We can improve this world,
Let's try to ride more bikes,
We can make things better,
Like giving animals back their rights.
We don't have to just sit there
And watch this Earth go down,
We can do anything we believe in.
We can stop the running,
Stop the screaming,
So we can have a peaceful night
And keep on dreaming.

Ameenah Arewa (11)
Sydenham School, Sydenham

BABY GENIUS

Truth

Every day I wake up
To the same monotonous routine,
Eat my beef and potato porridge,
Sit in front of a screen.

They don't seem to understand,
When I'm trying to speak,
Reciting the periodic table,
They're rocking me to sleep.

I don't think they can hear me,
Telling them about battles.
They just sit there cooing and ah-ing,
Shaking my toys and rattles.

Sometimes I get frustrated
And so I start to cry.
They think swinging me is helpful,
When I'm explaining pi.

They push me around in a trolley,
As if I can't walk.
It really is annoying
When they ignore me when I talk.

They put me to bed at 6 o'clock,
When I'm wide awake,
They think I'll give them a quiet night,
Well that's a big mistake!

Complaining to their friends
About how I'm never quiet.
So they *can* hear me,
When I tell them about my poor diet.

Always being patronised,
Never taken seriously,
People always staring,
Saying they want to steal me.

Being a baby is hard,
Every day is grey,
So next time you see one,
Listen to what they say.

Isla MacPhee (12)
Sydenham School, Sydenham

FEAR

Truth

Fear: the one real heartbreak,
It strangles you and surrounds you with darkness,
It takes you back to when you were young,
Death haunts your every move when fear's involved.

Darkness, death and fear hold hands
To welcome the Devil into their gang.
Fear creates monsters with claws
And fangs dripping with blood.
The place where you fight fear
Is filled with dead warriors.

Fight fear with friendship, with love, with kindness,
Fear makes your imagination go wild.
If you stand together,
If you help each other,
You may just win the battle of life.

The Devil laughs,
While tears rush like waterfalls from your eyes.
You surrender to fear.
The lord of darkness, the creature of night,
The dream crusher.
Seconds feel like hours,
Hours feel like days as the battle goes on.

Realise that fighting is wrong,
It's mean, it's bad with death involved.
Have love not hatred.
Forgiveness, friendship and love.
Think of happy memories,
Like leaves dancing in the autumn breeze,
Like fish swimming in the sea.
You can control fear,
After all, it's your feeling.

Fear itself is the real fear!

Evie Fraser Alderson (11)
Sydenham School, Sydenham

LIONS

Truth

Claws as sharp as a knife,
Fur as thick as a book
And teeth as dangerous as a snake.

Lions might seem very dangerous,
But really they are actually
Really cute and maybe sometimes
Harmless, depending on if you make them angry.

This animal is special because
It's really vicious but
Cute at the same time.
Not a lot of people know this
But lions are actually really playful.

They say a lion's roar
Can be heard five miles away.
Therefore, if you wake up one night
And you hear a lion's roar,
Which is completely different
From the old man's snore,
Don't panic, the lion could be
At least five miles away.

Then, on the other hand,
Maybe you should panic,
The lion could actually
Be only minutes away.

Lions laugh
Like jumping jaguars,
On top of talking trees.
When the talking trees start talking,
The joking jaguars fall off.

The lion,
He dwells in the waste,
He has a big head
And a very small waist,
But his shoulders are stark
And his jaws are grim
And a good little child
Will not play with him.

Nicole Kosiorek (11)
Sydenham School, Sydenham

THE MONSTER

Dare

A girl runs into school,
Face scratched and dripping blood,
Clothes torn and covered in mud.
She runs to the teacher
But they can't help with what is happening outside of school.

In the playground the girl hides in the dark.
She cowers in a corner trying not to be seen
By the terrible monster that taunts her.

At class she is safe,
But the moment the teacher steps out,
The bully towers over her.
No one looks,
No one speaks,
Why do they just sit there?
Why won't anyone stand up and help?

Twenty years into the future.
Where is the shy girl now?
Andy Jackson, the famous singer,
The girl who always hid behind her hair,
Now sings her heart away.
She sings about her traumatising childhood.

When she goes backstage,
She looks into her dressing room mirror
And sees the weedy girl that she used to be.
Memories of moments sad and bad
Fill her mind as she winces with pain.

One shake of her head.
Another look in the mirror.

Now she stands in a dazzling dress,
On every TV channel,
Singing to her heart's content.

Chiamaka Onumonu (11)
Sydenham School, Sydenham

DUNKIRK!

Truth

I waved him goodbye,
I gulped with sorrow,
My heart sank like quicksand,
I blinked, I looked up but he was gone.

I waved her goodbye,
Shaking like a leaf in fear.
I had to stay strong for her.
My face went rigid as I tried to blow a kiss.

I will miss the sound of her laughter,
Her adventurous eyes staring into me.
I will miss his strong arms holding me tight,
Oh, I do love him.

We marched up to the Spitfires.
I sat down and my head span with possibilities.
Suddenly, I got a flashback of her waving at me.

I strapped in and gripped tight
And flew up, up, up!
Whoop,
I looked down, armies of people standing as still as statues.
Bang!
A cannon shot!

All the birds flew away and their songs hushed
As the first war plane flew over our heads.
I just hoped he was OK,
But I knew he would be brave.

The engine went dead,
I was going down, down, down into the sea.
Goodbye, Mary.

I saw a plane going into the sea.
I hope that's not Daddy.

Crash!

Martha Simons (12)
Sydenham School, Sydenham

LIFE

Truth

A baby's first cry,
Turns into a smile,
As she gets held in her mother's arms.
Waah! Waah! Waah!
She starts crying again.

Crunch! Crunch! Crunch!
Goes the snow underneath her feet,
As she stumbles while she does her first steps.

Dringgggg!
Goes the dinging bell,
Telling everyone the school day has started.
The mother stays at the side of the gate
And whispers to her child, 'You'll do just great!'

'What's happening?' cried the child, looking up to her teacher.
'Just don't talk,' she replied and continued to talk to a doctor.
The only words she heard were:
Fall,
Cries,
Then silence.

Three weeks later,
Operation after operation,
As if a miracle had happened,
She started to walk again.
Check-up after check-up for several years,
She finally left her primary school six years later,
Feeling like she was leaving her family once again.
She said all her cries,
Then laters, goodbyes
And headed off to secondary.

Samiat Blessing Adediran (12)
Sydenham School, Sydenham

WHO AM I?

Truth

People think I am Indian
People think I am going to become a doctor because they think I am Indian
Well guess what? You're wrong
I am Sri Lankan, a person with feelings and emotions
Who am I?

People look at me strangely
The old lady on the bus looks at me weirdly
My teachers stare at me
Do they hate me?

In the Tamil community, I feel normal
The brightest, the craziest and the prettiest
In the English community, I feel uncomfortable
The ugliest, the darkest, the quietest
Where do I belong?

My colour gives me grief and stress
When I cough, everybody turns and looks
When somebody else burps they ignore it
I want to become a music director, I say
No, be a dentist and earn money
What am I, invisible?

People think I am Indian
People think I am going to become a doctor because they think I am Indian
Well guess what? You're wrong
I am Sri Lankan, a *woman* with feelings and emotions
Is that all I am?
Who am I?

Rasika Elangeswaran (11)
Sydenham School, Sydenham

WHAT GOD INTENDED

Dare

Answer me this, is this what God intended?
People questioning His name because of what we created
And us being too caught up in a virtual world to explain it
Because apparently sense is so overrated.

America seems to be falling to pieces,
Teaching hate to our nephews and nieces.
They say their country is complete,
Police do more to provoke this.
They put their hands on their heart,
Barack Obama was a start.
Then Trump came into the game
And tore us further apart,
But does race make us unequal?
Is that what God intended?
This world is broken and needs to be mended...

Britain's not perfect either.
It's far from that.
People are starving
With four kids in a council flat,
While the Queen sits on her throne,
With the option of being fat.
But does class really count?
Is that what God intended?

A world so constructed, disrupted and corrupted,
Has to be mended...

Nyobi Bassey (11)
Sydenham School, Sydenham

DOESN'T THIS BOTHER YOU?

Dare

Doesn't it bother you
That when you walk outside, the sky is grey,
Making our lungs turn black?
Doesn't it bother you
That we take water for granted
When there are people living in nothing but a shack?
Don't you feel a certain way,
Where you can go to school and back,
But somewhere in the world, people, evacuating,
Lying on the shores,
Because the way others treat others, I'm so bored
Doesn't it make you feel a certain way?
We must stop this, the people say.

Where did the animals go?
We imprisoned them just to be put on show,
Leaving them locked away.
Zoos won't release their animals, their state of living is low.
So many faults on the Earth and we live here,
We all need to get our points out in the clear.

If we all work together, we can connect the dots,
'Cause we all make friendship and peace.
Together we can make it,
Let's give it a shot.

Holly Yvonne Mary Whittington (12)
Sydenham School, Sydenham

WORDS CAN HURT

Truth

Words can hurt, make me feel sad,
When I haven't done anything bad,
Sometimes words that hurt the most,
Start as a joke or even a boast.

Words can hurt, drive me round the loop,
I don't like you and your group!
The words you say upset me,
Why can't you just let me be?

Words can hurt, ring in my ears,
I wish that I could tell my peers,
You bully me to look cool,
Don't you know you're just a fool?

Words can hurt, make me feel blue,
To be off school I fake the flu,
Even at break your gang hunts me down
Like a tiger, you make me frown.

Words can burn, I will not lie,
As I lie down at night and start to cry,
In my bedroom, my tears stream,
Why can no one hear my scream?

Words can hurt, make me cry,
Puts my heart in the sky,
Find the courage, speak up and tell,
Then maybe things will turn out well.

Maisie Newman (11)
Sydenham School, Sydenham

WOMEN'S WORLD

Dare

Let me tell a story,
It's about women's rights,
It may be strong and gory,
Why have we lost all our might?

What can we say,
About all this sexism,
It happens every day,
Don't get me started on racism.

'Oh no, you're black, mixed race, or even white!'
Every hour, second, we have to put up with this fight.
Maya Angelou, Rosa Parks, Beyoncé and her curls,
Who runs the world? Girls?

How come men get paid more?
Come on now, discrimination?
How will we find a cure?
We aren't waiting, we are not being patient.

This story I have told,
Let's hope it won't be true when I'm old.
Why are we being judged?
I'm not asking much.

Sexism, another woman hurt,
Haven't you learnt?

Is there such a thing as a 'girlie girl'?
Well, that's women's world.

Emily Grace Joanna Slanickova (11)
Sydenham School, Sydenham

SENSES

Dare

Today I see thick, grey smoke erupting from the tops of factories.
I watch humans argue over country and war.
Populations of beautiful animals shrink down to their thousands.

Today I smell thick oil leaking into our calm ocean.
Whiffs of cars' petrol finds its way up my nostrils, overpowering the brain.
Odours of money spin around as people steal from others.

Today I hear car engines driving through loud cities.
Thud! Trees hit the ground one after another.
I listen to terrible stories that have been spread across the news.

Today I taste food while others taste nothing.
Sugary foods leave a flavour in your mouth like a permanent pen.
Medicine slips down my throat to cure me from illness.

Today I touch my surroundings, getting warmer as the climate changes.
Rubbish skims me when I swim in the sea.
I feel sorry for the Earth. What did it do wrong?

Nell Rosie Wolstenholme (12)
Sydenham School, Sydenham

BEING BULLIED

Truth

It is my first day at school,
I walk through the gates,
The school bell rings and now I'm late.
Then some girls come looking very tall
And pick on me for being so small.

When I walk into class,
I'm feeling nervous and shy,
Then I drop all my things and everyone laughs.
I just want to cry.
A girl named Ella comes and comforts me,
She helps me pick up my things
And that makes me really happy.

Now it is break time and I eat my food.
The big girls return being even more rude.
Oh, how I wish this was all a dream,
Those bullies have taken my anger level to extreme.

I'm doing my work
And I am back at the top of the shelf,
Having fun with my friends, enjoying myself.
At the end of the day, I get pushed over like they don't care,
I want to get out of this living nightmare.

Hayat Abdi (11)
Sydenham School, Sydenham

SISTERSHIP

Dare

Look around you
What do you see?
People with a link
And no bond
They rage and they shout
Which creates war
When they could be nice
To make peace.

If we can care
The world will rejoice
Happiness will reign
Sister, be mine.

Why dislike?
Liking is better
It makes us nice
Which makes others happy
And makes us glad
Being related isn't breakable
Life is kinder
If we try to please.

If we can be nice
Our lives will rejoice

Peace will reign
Sister, be mine.

If one can be happy
And accept our sisters
Then we will not regret
The 3:20 bell
When we all go home
And have to spend
The next half day
With our siblings.

If we can be kind
Our hearts will rejoice
Love will reign
Sister.

I'll be yours
If you'll be mine.

Monifa Onitolo (11)
Sydenham School, Sydenham

AN ENVIRONMENT'S SONG

Dare

They say they're taking care of us
Yet they cut down trees
Pollute the air and water
And endanger animals' lives

They make cars and lorries
That pollute the air with waste
And cut down trees
To build factories in their place

They waste paper
And throw rubbish into the sea
They harm rainforests, reefs and rivers
With litter, pollution and gas

They destroy habitats
So animals have no place to give birth
They hunt and kill beautiful creatures
Till there are less and less on this Earth

It isn't right
All of it
Logging, hunting, polluting
Needs to stop

Before our beautiful world
Becomes nothing but a wasteland
Lush jungles cut down
Crystal-clear lakes reduced to sludge
Nothing will survive, not animals, not plants

So we need to change our ways
Before it's too late.

Jessica Mae Green (12)
Sydenham School, Sydenham

WHAT YOU DID

Dare

That girl you bullied,
You called her a daydreamer,
You said you'd be her friend
In her dreams.
Well guess what?
You are...

She is lying in her bed,
With a bottle of shoplifted sleeping pills.
She's dead.
That's what you did.

That man you teased,
You called him freaky
Because of his scars.
You told him to stay away,
So he does.

He never leaves his house,
He just sits on his old armchair,
Remembering the time
When he fought for his country.
Those bad memories,
You made him remember.

That girl you laughed at,
You called her a scaredy-cat.
You teased her about monsters
And the monsters came...

The monsters ate her that night,
Not fairy-tale monsters,
Monsters of sadness and anger.
They got too strong,
You led them to her.

That's what you did.

Kathryn Alice Hart (11)
Sydenham School, Sydenham

GONE

Truth

You were going to go one day or another,
Tedious pace was of the heart monitor.
Clouds were calling from above,
As slow as the flight of a dove.
Butterflies began to fly low,
Flowers began to fall.
Death had chosen you to follow,
My heart had hit a wall.

The things I knew you should have said,
Will always lie within my head.
The books I wrote but you never read,
Still are lying by my bed.
I feel my warm tears trickle down my face
And drop upon my hand,
You have broken down my happy place
And filled it with an unknown feeling of sad.

My sense of belief had blown away,
Drifted to another planet.
I think about you day by day,
How will I ever manage?
Like a fly amongst a swarm of bees,
I am cornered between two walls of fear.

You have brought me to my knees
And that will be the last that you will hear of me.

Hannah Oakey Adams (11)
Sydenham School, Sydenham

FAMILY

Truth

This is a poem about family.
There are big families, there are small families
And families in the middle.
Some families have one parent
And others have two.
There are families with children,
Families without.
There are grandparents, uncles,
Aunties and cousins.
Step-parents, real parents,
Adopted children, your children.
Loving families, awful families.
Annoying children, behaving children,
Jealous children, spoilt children,
They're all the same.
Abusive parents, new parents,
Some with no clue.
Pushy parents, gentle parents,
It's probably all new.
I have no more ideas,
So here's a quick clue,
Love your family,
But most important,
All families should love each other.

Would you like to live alone?
Probably not.
That's why you should respect your parents
And older siblings.

Alexandra Iwaniuk (11)
Sydenham School, Sydenham

WAR-TORN

Dare

My hand brushed against the water,
I wandered from the sea, wet to my waist,
The golden sand beneath my feet.
Bloodstained beyond recognition.
Ruined beyond belief.
I stared across the dunes and my heart stopped.

Like stars in the sky, like snow on the ground,
Bodies lay over the dunes.
Bitten in the jaws of the enemy.
Strangled in the arms of foe.
Blood dyed their jackets.
It confettied through their hair.
It splashed on their face.

Broken hearts and broken dreams washed away the land.
Beside the destroyed dunes,
The village cried for help.
Distant wails could be heard through the fog.
Children buried beneath buildings.
Adults under rubble.
Animals nowhere to be found.
I lay my head on the silent chest of a fighter.
She couldn't vote yet, but she could die in a war.
War-torn.

Ruby-Mae Kelly (12)
Sydenham School, Sydenham

THE LINE

Dare

Every day you ask if everything is OK,
Well, you get the same answer, 'Yes, I'm fine.'
Well you know it's not, so stand up and say 'Hey!'
It's not OK, you've just crossed the line.

Politics!
Prices are increasing,
Payments are decreasing,
More homeless, more weeping,
Terrorists bombing, shaking the land,
You know what? Why can't it just be banned?

Pollution!
Air escaping,
Toxins invading,
Ice melting,
Lives suffering,
Every day we get hurt,
Every day it gets worse,
Why can't we stop this terrible curse?

I have something to say to you,
Yes, all of you
Who answer 'It's fine,'
Has my explanation changed your state of mind?
We have all crossed the line.

Cara May Mulligan (11)
Sydenham School, Sydenham

CORRUPTION

Dare

A dim residential area
Lit by street lights, orbs of gold
Safety in the dark
Drunken steps follow in the shadows
Slurred mumbling
Then he felt the knife in his neck
A cold sharpness was softened by the blood
What did I do to deserve this?
Darkness

A lively area with friends
Laughter and love were alive
Jokes and cordiality
Shouts of disdain
Closer and closer
A gun to his head
Crying and pleading
Please don't shoot!
Shots fired
Darkness

A safe space with comrades
Peaceful and meaningful
A common goal in mind
A child, proud and free

Screams of hate
A uniform meant to protect
The child surrounded
Bludgeon after bludgeon in a pool of his blood
His ribs caved in
Tell my mother I love her!
Pain.

Dita Montgomery Kellett (11)
Sydenham School, Sydenham

MY PLANET

Dare

There is more than one planet
Different people believe in different things
And I believe in one.

This is a planet that no one will have guessed is
A planet of fun
A planet of laughter
And most importantly, a planet of green.

On this planet, people respect the environment
No one litters
No one fishes
No one chops the trees down.

But... let's face the real world
People are littering
People are fishing
People are chopping the trees down.

People think that the environment is nothing
Soon those people will see
The environment is everything
But when that happens, it will be too late to turn back...

You can't undo what you have done
You can't redo your mistake
You can see the history of the past
No one knows what the future holds.

Alena Hoangova (12)
Sydenham School, Sydenham

JUDGED

Dare

Since when
Was it awkward for a girl to love sports as much as a boy?
Since when
Was it OK to judge a person who knows and embraces they are gay at a young age?
Since when
Have men been known to apparently be stronger than women?
Since when
Did people get bullied or judged because of their race?
Since when
Was it OK to be hurt, or even worse, because of your religion?
Since when
Were people allowed to bully vulnerable people just because they are different?
Since when
Did young and old people of the world have no choice but to live on the streets helplessly?
Since when
Did teens and younger kids get so easily drawn into bad gangs which could ruin their future?
Since when
Did children get taken away by strangers without anyone noticing?

When will we all treat others as we would like to be treated?

Kaiya Beaton (12)
Sydenham School, Sydenham

FOR THOSE FUTURE GENERATIONS

Dare

Did you know the Amazon desert
Was once the Amazon rainforest?
It was once filled with trees but then...
People, humans, so-called citizens,
Cut them all down for one thing -
Money,
So for those future generations

Please forgive us for putting greed over love,
Calling destruction progress.
Now I know I am not the only one wanting to say sorry
Because...

That baby didn't start walking, talking
Without the help of his mum.
Shakespeare wasn't born with paper
And a quill in his mouth.
No!
He worked to get from point A to point B.

Didn't Martin Luther King have a dream?
Don't we?
So for those future generations,
Plant your tree so it can become more than a seed,

So...

Dear future generations...
Sorry.

Caitlin Clarkson (11)
Sydenham School, Sydenham

LEAVING YOU

Truth

The day I left you
I wish it had never come
I put on my shoes
Packed my bag
And went

I couldn't bear the sound of every chug
Chugging away from home
Wondering where I'll go
Wondering where I'll get to
My heart thumping out of my life
That sound is bumping
Leaving you

The feeling
That feeling
Those feelings
Of loneliness
I am lonely
That ugly feeling
Of being without you
Leaving you

My child doesn't know
I feel guilty
As guilty as ever
She wakes up
Calling my name
Calling for a game
Those good times

As my tears fall
I remember
What she will do
I know she will shed those same tears
At that same place
At that same time
As I do
Leaving you
Leaving you.

Eleanor Chambers (11)
Sydenham School, Sydenham

MY CAT AND ME

Truth

Sometimes I sit and watch,
My cat playing with socks.
She eats her food from a pot,
Then sicks out the entire lot.
I wake up with my cat on my face,
Then she runs off for mice to chase.
As a little bug flies by,
She makes a sound like she's going to cry.

I'm sure you've figured out,
No doubt,
From this,
My cat is full of stupidness.
I wonder what I'd be like as a cat,
Doing catty things of this and that…

Another day and another week,
Being a cat has no fun streak.
Prowl around, wait for food,
Nothing changes my cat-grumpy mood.
I watch as humans do their chores
And use their sofas for my claws.
They do nothing I wish to see,
Except being butlers for me.

Eat,
Sleep,
Repeat.

Beatrice Rutherford (11)
Sydenham School, Sydenham

WHAT HAD TO CHANGE

Dare

Earlier on this day,
I decided what had to change,
It wasn't the lush green grass
Or my window's clear glass,
It was the world.

Now I know that nobody's perfect,
But here's a few things that can change,
From self-respect to child neglect,
I knew we could all change that
Because that's no maths.

But I thought that the two things
That really had to change were
Racism and sexism.
Maybe I sound petty,
Maybe I sound like a crazy whisperer.

It had to change,
I tried all I could,
But nobody would
Listen to me,
So I decided on something.

I made a change,
I decided that people make mistakes,
And sometimes it's OK to let it be,
But I would always remember
What had to change.

Isabella Mensah (11)
Sydenham School, Sydenham

FREEDOM

Truth

The twinkle of stars and the sprinkles of moondust,
I wonder what freedom is like?
I dance in an ocean of night,
My feet move swiftly and softly as I dance in winter.
This freedom, this freedom is perfect,
I listen to the birds singing to their chicks,
And hear water running down a stream.

Suddenly, I am running as fast as lightning,
I do not dare to look back.
Is freedom that terrifying?
I come to a river and meet a hummingbird
That says to me,
'Are you OK? Come in, come in,
I will keep you warm.'
I go inside his house and fall asleep.
I wake up and it was all a dream.

Ding! went the sleeping clock,
I danced quietly and quickly up a hill
And I watched the stars wink at me.
This is what I call freedom.

Nina Funa Visser (11)
Sydenham School, Sydenham

WORLD WAR I

Dare

War, conflict, injury, death,
All the things you don't want to hear,
All the people who have died for their country,
Giving up to them what is dear.

Trauma, fear, anxiety, despair,
They now regret what they have done,
For believing in the 'We need you' sign
And joining World War I.

Worry, terror, panic, dread,
Of the families of the fighting,
Thinking that every day,
Their loved one is dying.

Starving, skinny faces of the poor,
Helplessly, hopelessly begging,
Trying to survive the relentless war,
And the sadness it is bringing.

Now that is over, now that is done,
No one remembers the pain,
Of the people who fought,
The people who suffered,
The wrath of World War I.

Sylvia Sheppard (11)
Sydenham School, Sydenham

MY BIG BAG OF BULGING WORRIES

Truth

I woke up one morning,
I checked the time,
I thought to myself,
It would be just fine
And as I got dressed
Into my new secondary school uniform,
I skipped out of the house and waved goodbye.
I then got to the school gates
And took a deep, deep breath.
I ran behind a tree and cried,
'OMG, what if I get bullied?
What if I get super shy?
What if I confess to a new crush
And he makes my heart die?'
I opened my bag to get my phone,
But when I did,
Oh, you'll never guess what I found!
I found 20,000,000
Big bags of bulging worries,
Attempting to surround.

I fall to the ground,
I suddenly blink at myself,
I run to the school gates
And tell my beautiful self,
'I've got this!'

Anya Nwakaego Umeh (11)
Sydenham School, Sydenham

WHAT HAS THIS WORLD COME TO?

Dare

Social media!

Nowadays people use it
To judge and cyberbully.

Once you post, the next thing you know
It's gone viral.

Texting and saying you're alright
When you are really crying inside.

People blackmailing and controlling you
Leading you in a direction that is not your destiny.

Confusing you
And making you feel unimportant.

Telling you they are someone
That they are not.

Criticising you for who you are
How you dress and what you do.

When children are fighting
Why is a phone the first thing to pick up and video
Instead of stopping the fight?

What has this world come to?
Hmm, social media.

Ayodele Afful (12)
Sydenham School, Sydenham

EYES OF THE WORLD

Truth

My eyes are wandering around and around,
My head is spinning like this world.
Life is a rush of emotions,
Each one never-ending.

I've been to so many places,
Seen so many faces, some sad,
Some lost and others
That just don't seem to care.

Every day someone dies,
Then another is born.
So with miracles like this,
Why do we continue to mourn
And scare and tease,
When others can't hear
The splash of clean water,
Can't smell fresh food upon the table,
Can't feel the warmth of a caring home,
And can't see the ones they love.

So I want you to stop,
Think and look at the world around you,
See through another's eyes,
Be glad to be alive.

Mauve Emerald Roslynd Mawston (11)
Sydenham School, Sydenham

WHY WAR?

Dare

Why the war and the fight?
Why dark and not light?
Why is the world full of hate?
Why do some think others are less great?
Why war?

Countries,
They bicker over ridiculous things,
Like what parts of the world are their belongings.

Friends,
This is mine and this is yours,
Then there's the fight and they are friends no more.

Race,
Some people are judged on their skin, even their hair,
And are treated with bullying or a mean glare.

Sex,
Why do some think girls have to keep their hair long
And why do some think pink for a boy is just wrong?

Why do we fight? I don't understand,
Why can't we be hand in hand?

Why?
Why war?

Mika Eilon (11)
Sydenham School, Sydenham

ALONE

Truth

I felt like a star alone in the empty night
I felt like a dot that wasn't part of anything
True love stays
But people leave
Time flies as people die
I'll miss you
Every time I see you
You are not there
I feel devastated
Friendship bonds frozen
As people doze into their death
My memories are spent thinking about you
Where are you?
Darkness looms around me
When will I see you again?
You make me smile
But when you vanish I cry
Our love stays
But you are gone
So I cry
You hear me while I cry
But please come today
The ocean's crying
And I am watching you

In every dream
I try to see you
But it's like a shield blocking you
When will I see you again?

Maryam Bah (11)
Sydenham School, Sydenham

SHE AND HE

Dare

Why does she do this?
Why does he do that?
Why can't we do what we want?

Is she weak?
Is he strong?
Is she kind?
Is he aggressive?
Is she passive?
Is he dominant?
Are these stereotypes really true?

Why does she like fashion?
Why does he like football?
Why does she like gymnastics?
Why does he like gaming?
Why does she like gossiping?
Why does he like skateboarding?
Why is it so unfair?

Why is she a nurse?
Why is he a policeman?
Why is she a teacher?
Why is he a businessman?
Why is she a hairdresser?

Why is he a plumber?
Why is it so unequal?

Why does she do this?
Why does he do that?
We need to make a change!

Isabella Caseley (11)
Sydenham School, Sydenham

FRIENDSHIPS

Truth

Friends are everything
Or are they nothing?
Being friends
Making friends
Having friends
What's the difference?

Maybe your best friend
Was your best friend
That doesn't make you nothing.
I don't like seeing people on their own

They have friends
Who have friends
Of friends of my friends
Who are friends of friends...
Ugh, stop!
It is too confusing

Life can be a bubble
When the time comes, it pops!
You'll fall and fall, then be in a cage
Locked up like a precious bird
They will treat you like rubbish

But at the start...
You're the star of the show
At the end, you are an endless, lonely black hole.

Rumaysah Z Saeed (11)
Sydenham School, Sydenham

NATURE DANGER!

Dare

Poaching is bad, just stop,
Yeah, imagine you're there,
You've done nothing wrong,
Then *bang, bang, bang,* you're dead.
Taken to the butchers for meat,
Next day, bought,
Then gobbled up in a blink.

Oceans and rainforests,
Deserts and mountains,
Savannahs and rivers,
Used to be full of life,
But now *empty!*
They're empty
Because of us.
We kill them in one shot.
We have them as food,
But imagine a place of peace,
No meat.

Imagine a giant coming towards you with a gun,
They kill your friends but you hide.
How would you feel?

All your mates, dead.
And now you,
One shot, you're gone too.

Ruby Bremner (11)
Sydenham School, Sydenham

THEIR GAME

Dare

Presidents and parliament, kings and queens
Tell us who we are and what to do
And nobody questions them
So who will tell them
We are not all a piece in their games?

You are more than a nobody
But that's what the rulers label us
When they send missiles at each other
Thinking only of themselves
Not of humanity, lying to get the vote
Saying what people want to hear
Not the brutal truth, not reality
But when someone finds out the truth
People cover their ears and won't accept it
That is when we become a piece in their game.

We are all stronger than they believe
Smarter than we are given credit for
Because if we don't question authority,
Who will?

Ella Sinnott-Behrmann (11)
Sydenham School, Sydenham

GIRL POWER

Dare

When you look around, what do you see?
Girls like you and me,
That have a right to say, 'We are strong,'
Without boys saying,
'Boys are better than girls!'

When you look around, what do you see?
Girls like you and me,
That have a right to play a sport like football
Without boys saying,
'Boys are better than girls!'

When you look around, what do you see?
Girls like you and me,
That have a right to say 'We are clever,'
Without boys saying,
'Boys are better than girls!'

When you look around, what do you see?
Girls like you and me,
That have the right to say,
'We can do whatever we want in the world!'

Maya Reuben (11)
Sydenham School, Sydenham

WHAT HAVE WOMEN DONE TO DESERVE THIS?

Dare

Men say women aren't enough
But us women are powerful
So give it up
Men can be sporty
So can we
So please just let us be.
We are like butterflies on our way
Men are like cheaters cheating their way.

Women don't deserve to be the worst
Men can be leaders
So why can't we?
They make the rules
We follow them through.
Why can't it be the other way round?
Come on, give us a chance.

Women do the washing
We also do the cleaning
Men do the fighting
Always at war.

We could be the leader
We're strong too!
Change the plan for once
Let us lead the crew.

We are women
Fighting for who we really are.

Sharia Cherryanne Pascal (11)
Sydenham School, Sydenham

HOME AWAY

Dare

Run, run, run!
Nowhere to go, running as fast as a cheetah,
Breath is running out,
I have to go back, I told myself,
But in my head I can't stop, just keep going.
At home, Mum is screaming to Dad about war.
What is war?
I ask myself what is war?
Two countries disagree and then war starts.
What is the point?
Now I stop running,
Dad is risking his life for his country.

I start to see something,
All this time it was blurry,
But something touches me... now!
An ice-cold hand touches my shoulder,
Who on earth could it be?

One year later,
Buried in a grave,
Never saw the person who killed me,
But I am dead
And the dead can't live again.

Emma Winter (11)
Sydenham School, Sydenham

SYRIANS SUFFERING

Dare

Somewhere in the world these people suffer,
As we live the life we love,
Poor souls are killed by powerful people,
Children search for their worried families.

Deafening sounds; the last thing they hear,
The wind gushes across their face,
As bullets dig into their skin,
Stealing souls from innocent lives.

Blood erupts, covering towns in red,
Screams are mostly heard echoing from far,
The smell of smoke drifts into the air,
Families hurry to the safety of other countries.

Parents can do nothing but watch and mourn as their children die,
Children wail when friends and family pass,
Who suffers this badly in life?
Syrians suffer, striving for their life.

Fawzia Ali (11)
Sydenham School, Sydenham

STAND UP FOR WHAT YOU BELIEVE IN!

Dare

Tearing families apart,
Who will be persuaded?
Once a solid nation!
What happened?
Just over a year ago,
Everyone was happy and united.

Why are people allowed to protest?
There's only one person you had to ask.
Protesting must be stopped! Now!
Protesting can't be accepted.
This nation cannot even pull a deal together.
Stand up for what you believe in.
When was the last time
You stood up for what you believe in?

What can you do? Believe in yourself.
Theresa May is not the one at fault.
No one believed in her.
We can make this right.

We need to pull together as a nation.
Make this right.
Don't let there be another.

Lauren George-Wood (11)
Sydenham School, Sydenham

WOMEN'S RIGHTS

Dare

It's not a subject everyone talks about,
But it is more important than you guess.
How would you feel if men cared about you less?
Then an event happened which changed lives for all us women.

Grouping together, women changed the rules,
Proving that the men were the fools,
To not let us vote,
I don't like to gloat,
But we change the elections.

We tied ourselves to the railings of Big Ben,
We stayed there until ten,
On the streets we protested,
The police detected,
That we were not going to give up
And we didn't.

So when taking part in votes,
Think of us women,
Who protested against men
And brought us so far.

Heidi Elizabeth Leon Quezada (12)
Sydenham School, Sydenham

WHAT IS RACISM?

Dare

People make comments about people's race
It does mean they come from that place
Why are people racist?
Who are these type of people?
Are they being judged?

This isn't fair
People cannot do the things they want
These people just do not care
People need to stand up for themselves
People get freedom
People get nothing.

This is important
We are all being judged by somebody
But secretly.
If you are reading this and you are racist
Stop!
It is not funny
It is not a game.

What would happen if this carries on?
Will one race keep on going?
Will everybody else die in tragedy?
Please stop racism.

Maariya Maya Alom (11)
Sydenham School, Sydenham

WORLD WAR 2

Truth

Wave goodbye
Holding back my tears
Can't turn back
Wish Dad the best of luck

Rolled back and forth in my bed
Bang, crash, tears, screams
I'm scared to the brink
Can't turn back
Still wishing Dad the best of luck

The next day a letter came
Mom slides down a pole
'Why are you crying?' I ask when she's in bed
'Darling, Dad's dead!'

Tears roll down my cheeks
I don't believe it's true
I wonder if...
Shaking my head, don't have a clue

I was walking through the woods
When I see Dad limping towards me
Won't turn back
Dad used my luck.

Aaisho Buule (11)
Sydenham School, Sydenham

LOCKED AWAY

Dare

Locked away,
I'm locked away in my dark room,
Locked away,
I'm locked away from the outside world,
Locked away,
No contact, no friends, alone,
A secret to all existence.

Bang! The front door slams.
Crash! The keys slap the counter top.
Stomp! Stomp! Stomp!
The shadow of my abuser.
My usual tear streams down my face,
Close after, another from the other eye
Shoots down my face like a river
Trying to get revenge.
I could tell today would be one of the worst.
The smell of weed and alcohol
Drifts past my nose.
I lie down in my bed, hoping and praying
I won't lie back here with bruises...

Sophia George-Pendleton (12)
Sydenham School, Sydenham

ANOTHER WORLD

Dare

It's normal to be different
Challenge yourself
Put yourself out there
Make the change to what you believe in
Be thoughtful of what you say
Let your actions be seasoned with love
Stand up, speak out
Don't keep what you think is wrong to yourself
It's not about race, it's not about colour
Treat others how you want to be treated yourself
Let's not segregate, let's not separate
Equal access and opportunity for all
Embrace the difference that you see
Stand up, speak out
Make the world a better place
For those around you
Stop war, stop racism
Let your actions bring peace
It's normal to be different
Challenge yourself.

Savannah Wood (11)
Sydenham School, Sydenham

RACISM

Dare

Something I hate the most
That makes me angry and sad
Is racism that spreads like a disease
It can bring families to their knees.

It is evil and wrong
But people are tagging along
To this terrible thought
That leaves families fraught.

It is wrong to think differently about people
It is wrong to judge by skin colour
It is wrong to assume by religion
It is wrong to hurt people because of their beliefs.

In this day
People are being killed
And the population will build
On this monstrous minefield.

Everyone is equal
We are all the same
The world needs to be peaceful
And there should be no shame.

Emily Barker (11)
Sydenham School, Sydenham

A GIRL'S WORLD

Dare

When a girl wears trousers to school
The boys act like it's against the rules
Boys think they're better at handling tool kits
And girls belong making cakes at markets

They think that girls belong in heels
And at home cooking their meals
Us girls are practically treated like slaves
It's like an endless maze

You're trying and trying to find your way out
But the boys are the bushes, cutting you off and pushing you about
Girls are gifted and giving
Some of the words that boys call us are unforgiving

Because girls are strong!
Because girls are smart!
We will fight all day long
And we will go very far!

Iris Kemp (11)
Sydenham School, Sydenham

THE RAIN AND ME

Truth

I like rain,
I just do,
Earlier the rain came,
So, we withdrew.
Loving the rain is insane,
So they say,
But I believe there's another way.

A way people can see the rain as beautiful,
A way people can see the rain like the sun,
A way the rain could bring joy everywhere,
The people would rejoice that the rain had come,
There would be banners, food, laughter and fun.

That's just a dream,
But only for now,
So, I will wait until it's my turn to speak,
Until then, you won't hear a peep.

But while I sit here,
Gently brushing the tear-covered window,
I wonder,
Why do I love the rain?

Jessica Ansbro (11)
Sydenham School, Sydenham

DANCE IS MY LIFE

Truth

Dance is my life, my heart, my soul,
I dance for no one but myself.
I waltz down the corridors,
I tap dance around the hall,
I never lose, I either win or learn.

Dance is my life, my heart, my soul,
Ballet fills me with joy,
I pirouette and chasse around the house,
In search of more ways to fly.

Dance is my life, my heart, my soul,
I could write this poem all night,
But although no one knows how far I go,
I'd really just like to dance.

Dance is my life, my heart, my soul,
I can win this audition,
But if I don't,
Please don't gloat,
Because I never lose, I either win or learn.

Lola Capstick (11)
Sydenham School, Sydenham

ENVIRONMENT

Dare

Walking down the street, you could sense a horrible smell,
So you turn to your left, the right, just to see litter and empty bottles.
Rolling across the ground.
Spit everywhere, what is wrong with us?
Where has our hygiene gone? Are we even humans now?
You would imagine a spotless, stainless street, but no,
All we can see is our stinky, smelly trash.
We need fresh air, not contaminated air!
This is a disgrace to our human name.

We are like wild animals, but even worse...
I thought humans were smart,
Well I guess we aren't when the subject of our environment comes up.
Then we all turn into frozen and brainless statues.

Xia Lin (11)
Sydenham School, Sydenham

WHY BULLY ME?

Truth

People will forget what you've said to them,
People will forget what you've done to them,
A number of people,
Who will never forget how you made them feel...

A new beginning, a whole new world,
Something lies ahead, but hasn't been told...

She gives you an evil eye,
You want to ask why.
She points at you, laughing with pride,
You get an emotional feeling inside...

The next day she would call you names,
You think that she should get the blame.
She punches you and you fall down,
You cry, she got the crown...

Bully wins once again,
All you wanted was a friend.

Lillian Terletska (11)
Sydenham School, Sydenham

MEMORIES

Dare

My primary school was full of banter
Like the time my friend tried to sneak in Fanta
I miss my old teacher, Miss Perkins
I remember how she hated gherkins.
I even miss the dinner ladies!
They used to argue in the background in assembly
I clearly remember the head teacher, Miss Eko
All the kids would echo, echo, echo her
I wonder how my friends are getting on
I wonder if they remember our friendship song…

A memory that will stay in my memories
Is when we did Charlie and the Chocolate Factory
And how Year 6 worked together like a big family
I think I'm going to end my poem here
In case I shed a tear.

Tiana Foster (11)
Sydenham School, Sydenham

COLOURS

Dare

He may be black and she may be white,
Yet there is some huge gap in-between.
We are born different colours and that should define us?
Funny, people may think that,
Yet what black people see, white people see
And so does everyone else in the world.

We think that our world has changed so much,
And everything is 'good'.
Without thinking, people make assumptions,
Say racist things here and there,
But they are just 'joking'.

Think of all the bad things in the world,
What's the cause?
Race!

We need to unite,
Stand strong,
We come from the same origin.

Izzi Phillips (11)
Sydenham School, Sydenham

THE WAR

Dare

A field,
A lush green field,
The flowers,
The beautiful flowers,
The grass,
The freshly cut spring grass,
The trees,
The trees swaying in the distance,
Like they're trying to communicate,
But no one is there to listen.

A field,
A broken field,
The flowers,
The bloody flowers,
The grass,
The grass with soulless bodies in the middle of it,
The trees,
The shot trees crying blood, lie still,
The field is no more,
It's been taken over by war,
Nothing's left apart from blood, sweat and fear,
And families left in tears,
The war has been here.

Ellie-Mae Hogan (11)
Sydenham School, Sydenham

WHAT'S HAPPENING TO THE WORLD?

Dare

What's happening to the world,
Oh, what's happening to the world?
It's as if we don't know right from wrong,
Or how to stop and change what went on.

I think sometimes we forget just how others feel,
Until they reveal a glimpse of a tear.
But still some of us feel it's OK to be cruel,
When only if they knew how it felt to be treated like a mule.
They would see it for themselves,
Which is why I need your help to show the world what we have become.

What's happening to the world,
Oh, what's happening to the world?
What I hope's happening
Is a change!

Olivia-Jean Imaga (11)
Sydenham School, Sydenham

MASKS

Truth

People hide their emotions, pushing them to one side,
Others, blind as bats, don't see them suffering behind their lies.

The girl who may be sweet, happy and light,
May be the girl who cries herself to sleep at night.

For all these lies we say to hide the truth,
These masks we hide behind are like intricate tattoos.

Ones that tell stories that are missing locks to a key,
Or the painful sting of a wild bumblebee.

So please don't hide behind this mask,
Look out for other people and ask.

Could you help me come from behind my
Emotionless mask?

Leela West (11)
Sydenham School, Sydenham

A LIFE WITHOUT BEES

Dare

Buzz
Buzz
Buzz
Stop
Silence...

As time passed, things began to get frightening
The plants died and the trees slowly faded
No fish, no cows, no fresh green grass
No colourful flowers
And no bees.

Wherever I go,
I hear dead trees swaying and creaking in the hot wind.
Constantly, rusty, rotten dead people dropping on the ground
Daily, choking and screaming people dying all around
I see wild, angry, crackling fire slowly consuming the world.
Everywhere there is a misty, fuzzy dust, all over my body...

Like a grubby blanket.

Dotty Burdett (12)
Sydenham School, Sydenham

ENVIRONMENT

Dare

Nature is a wonderful and beautiful thing.
The Amazon rainforest is being cut down,
Animals are losing their homes.
I am wondering who are those people doing this?
And why?
Would you like your homes to be destroyed?
This is happening to animals in the Amazon rainforest!

People are killing animals for fun,
Putting animal heads on walls for decorations,
Using their fur for rugs and carpets.
People cut off rhino horns and sell them for lots of money.
It is cruel, animals are part of this world too!
There are many endangered animals in this world,
So let's help them live!

Roberta White (11)
Sydenham School, Sydenham

TRUTH ABOUT SOCIAL MEDIA

Truth

Why are people bullying online?
Maybe they have nothing else to do.
They might not have any friends to talk to.

Firstly, when someone sends you a hurtful message,
It feels like you are buried deep in the ocean.

He might be a stranger,
He might be a thief,
You don't know who they are,
They tell another lie.

She might be a stranger,
She might be a thief,
You don't know who they are,
They tell another lie.

Don't listen to them,
You don't know if they are telling the truth.

Always tell an adult!

Tia George-Flavius (11)
Sydenham School, Sydenham

WHY ARE WE SELFISH?

Truth

When you peer around, what do you see?
A world that's empty
And nothing happy.
There are no more trees, they have been chopped down
And all of the flowers have been picked up and chucked down
And all of the animals, they are gone, they are far.

All the tigers are now decoration,
There is no more life,
No more inspiration,
There is no more colour,
It's all been faded out.
I thought life was exciting,
That's what it's all about.

There is nothing to see,
Not even a flying bee.
It's all vanished,
Because we are selfish.

Beatrice Lily Seaton (11)
Sydenham School, Sydenham

EVERYDAY-ISM

Dare

Racism, sexism, what else is there to say?
What has the world come to this day?
Bang... another one gone
Could this world have been perfect all along?

Everyday-ism, we're losing our pride
Every five seconds someone has died.

Everyday-ism, we're losing our women
Because they are being criticised, even though they have tried.

Everyday-ism, there is a lot of discrimination
Racism? Really?
Can't we be nice?
Do we have to continue this fight?

Racism?
Sexism?
That's what we call everyday-ism.

Amy-Rose Louisa Masic (12)
Sydenham School, Sydenham

THE DRAGON OF THE FOREST

Truth

I was walking through the forest one day,
When I saw a magnificent sight.
A creature ever so big and bold,
Stretched out its wings and took flight.
It flew ever so high, up to the sky,
Then suddenly it swooped down to me,
Through the trees, narrowly passing by.

Scales green like envy,
Claws black as coal,
Teeth that seemed the opposite of friendly,
It could easily crunch a mole.
The dragon of the forest,
Is definitely the hottest,
So when you're walking through the forest,
Look out for this beast,
Or you'll be his next dragon feast.

Faith Esther Grace (11)
Sydenham School, Sydenham

THE WAVES OF LYMINGTON

Truth

I'm running along the shore with my dog's lead in my hand,
We are both making footprints in the grainy sand.
My golden-brown hair flowing out behind me,
As my eyes are connecting with the sea.
These are the waves of Lymington,
My waves of Lymington.

My wellies are splashing up the sea,
Whilst my mum and grandad watch me.
They laugh and watch my dog and I,
I feel like I'm soaring through the sky.
The salty breeze chills my bones,
But as I'm filled with joy it's barely known.
These are the waves of Lymington,
My waves of Lymington.

Abbigail Grima (11)
Sydenham School, Sydenham

TEACHERS

Dare

We can't live with them
We can't live without them
They are so bossy
They ask if everything is OK
No! Nothing is OK!
Teachers are so mean
Why do we need teachers?
Why can't we be home-schooled?
Why don't we live our lives?
We don't need teachers' help
Why is it when we need help they come up to us?
Teachers just get us into trouble
Teachers moan every single morning
Why do we have rules in school?
School is boring
Some people get bullied, teachers do nothing
Why do we even have school?
When will school ever end?

Halia Bakare (11)
Sydenham School, Sydenham

BULLY WINS AGAIN

Dare

My life was perfect
Until the frown
The bully came along
With a cunning growl.
I tried to back away
Slowly I staggered
The bully and her posse
They began to look daggers.

Into a classroom I tried to run
But my shoes were stuck to the floor
They rubbed their hands together
Then they slammed the door
I wouldn't leave without a fight
But I was overwhelmed with fright.

But I shoved them out of the way
I cried all the way home
The bully wins the fight
Yet another day
I think this bullying is to stay.

Vishranthie Prapakaran (11)
Sydenham School, Sydenham

BULLY!

Truth

Bully,
I got bullied,
Bullies are not nice,
Did you get bullied?
Well here and now,
I'm going to sing you a rhyme.

They make you feel lost,
They make you feel scared,
Well, you're not lost or scared
Because someone will always be there.

You make it right,
Because they are just trying to pick a fight.
You're better than what they make out you are,
So don't drain yourself out
And just fill yourself with joy.
So there are bullies for you,
Now sort them out before they try and sort you.

Kirsty Louise Barnes (11)
Sydenham School, Sydenham

ENDANGERED ANIMALS

Dare

Why do humans harm animals?
I wonder if there's a reason why.
Imagine a world without animals...
I think I'm about to cry.

There would be deserted rainforests,
Oceans and forests all around the world,
Different animals are endangered,
Such as otters, bears, beetles,
Big cats and birds.

It is sad that humans shoot elephants
And rhinos for ivory
And then carve it for jewellery.
How unfair is that?
The biggest living creature on Earth
Is the blue whale,
But sadly now endangered.
This must stop!

Olivia Juutilainen (11)
Sydenham School, Sydenham

A STRAY

Dare

Woof! A swift kick on the rib
Miaow! A wine bottle to the leg

Humans are betraying
Dogs are hesitating
Cats are entertaining

An innocent body, small and scrawny
Walking helplessly down the street
A soft, meaningful voice bellows out of its mouth
But we hear nothing at all.

A small bark, a small miaow
Lost in the evil world of humans

Some people think that dogs and cats are worth nothing, nothing at all
But helping dogs and cats means something, something not so small.

Libby Alcock (11)
Sydenham School, Sydenham

THE WORLD IS AT WAR

Truth

A grey and motionless day
Lightly the rain pours away
The sun is asleep behind the clouds
The world moves on without a sound

All are happy except for one
Her dreams have been shattered
Her feelings are done
No more emotions for the thing she loved
Why, oh why has this been done?

What was the thing she loved so dear?
Come a bit closer and I'll tell you here
The simple thing she prayed for
Was world peace and nothing more
But then she realised it cannot be done
The world is at war with everyone.

Eva Harris (11)
Sydenham School, Sydenham

LIFE IS A TELENOVELA

Truth

Life is a telenovela,
All the things I've been through,
All the things I had to say to be here today,
Life is a telenovela.

I'm in a boat in the middle of the ocean,
Surrounded by sharks,
All on my own.
My boat is sinking just like my heart,
The sun is setting, it's a work of art.
Then all of a sudden, a shadow appears,
He saves my life, I'm shaking with fear.

Life is a telenovela,
I don't know his name
But he saved me, he saved my life,
He is my one true love, mi amor.

Kira Spencer Brown (11)
Sydenham School, Sydenham

LIES

Truth

Lies, people hate them,
But why do they spread them?
When people hide the truth from you
And tell a lie to cover up,
Do you think that lie is true?
Are white lies OK to tell so long as they protect?
Do we fall apart or connect?
People get mad and cry.
Why did they lie?

The reason why we lie differs.
When it comes out... it's bitter.
We deal with it through aches and pain,
Who is to blame?
Sometimes you feel like you want to die,
But if you hold your head high,
You will fly past the lie.

Jennifer Nguyen (11)
Sydenham School, Sydenham

FINDING MONEY

Dare

I go to the shops,
One day it's expensive,
One day it's not.
How can I live, how can I survive
With simple food so expensive?

I can't afford it, I need to move
Away from here,
But everywhere I go it's the same.
Life is hard, jobs don't pay,
Still there's no escape.
You ask for your change,
And you don't get it back,
How can we live our lives like that?

No more money,
No more food,
Are we going to beat this
Or are we going to lose?

Naomi Walters-Collett (11)
Sydenham School, Sydenham

FRIENDS 4 LIFE

Truth

When my friends are with me,
I can be happy,
I can be sad
And even sometimes a little mad.
Cos they know me so well,
They would never judge.

We love to make slime,
Cos slime is the best,
We keep on trying,
Even if it isn't a huge success.

Sleepovers rule.
We watch films,
We trade phones,
We eat treats,
We tell spooky stories
And we eat loads of sweets.

We hang in the park,
We make videos and dances,
Like we're super stars.

Isabella Jones (11)
Sydenham School, Sydenham

A RAINBOW

Truth

R ed, orange, yellow, green, blue, pink and purple all join to create magic
A beautiful way of expressing colours
I t's interesting how a rainbow can be formed by rain and shine
N obody has ever found the pot at the end of the rainbow
B ut I'm pretty sure there is one
O f all the wonderful things in the world, a rainbow has to be the most obvious one for people to recognise
W ow! That's what all the children and parents say when they see a rainbow.

Fienna Isabella Santos De Jesus (12)
Sydenham School, Sydenham

RAIN

Truth

Rain is falling from the sky
Pitter-patter, pitter-patter
The clouds go grey
Pitter-patter, pitter-patter
I hear the wind whistle
Pitter-patter, pitter-patter
As white puffs shed tears
Pitter-patter, pitter-patter
I feel the drops land on my hand as they start to fade away
Pitter-patter, pitter-patter
I taste the minerals as my tongue absorbs the salty water
I love the rain and the puddles as we stomp together in a great big huddle.

Sahar Azimi (11)
Sydenham School, Sydenham

FIGHT FOR WHAT YOU BELIEVE IN

Truth

The earth is dry and dusty,
The ocean is wet and soggy.

The air is as cold as Antarctica,
The animals are as extinct as dinosaurs.

Bomb! There goes the last tree down,
Bomb! There goes the last elephant killed.

The earth is dry and dusty,
The ocean is wet and soggy.

The humans are dead and gone,
Kaboom! The last human has disappeared.

What shall we do now
To save our planet?

Victoria Odaranile (11)
Sydenham School, Sydenham

WHAT HAVE WE DONE?

Dare

The oceans are filled with dirt and rubbish,
No wonder people don't go and see it.
The forest of deafening sounds are now silent,
No predators hunting for their prey,
No animal to be found.
Where are they?
Where have they gone?
They are nowhere to be seen.
What have we done?
The oceans used to be filled with many fish,
But now it is just dirt and trash
Because we don't take care of our stuff.
We destroy other animals' homes.
What have we done?

Michaela Dadzie (11)
Sydenham School, Sydenham

WINNER

Dare

Winners might not want to win, but they refuse to lose,
Winners know that you don't get what you wish for,
Winners know that you only get what you work for,
Winners know that if you fall over, you need to get back up,
Winners know that you can't win straight away,
Winners know that working hard causes a lot of blisters and bruises,
Winners know that it isn't you versus them, it's you versus you,
Winners know that they are the winners and they will never lose!

Francesca Vass Redford (11)
Sydenham School, Sydenham

THE RACIST BULLY

Dare

Every school morning, I walk down the same old crossing
I hear loads of people screaming and shouting
Some whispering
Smug faces, smirking, glancing around
Whispering
Prejudiced remarks
Unkind comments
But loud enough for someone to hear
I want to say don't be afraid
Of people like that
No matter where you are from
Or what you look like
Be proud
Look the smirking faces in the eye
And shout
'I am proud of me!'

Zahra Mughal (11)
Sydenham School, Sydenham

YESTERDAY ON REPEAT

Truth

How would a gramophone represent your past?
Would it replay all the happy memories, friendships and laughs?
Or would the speakers play all the unsaid things that just won't go away?
All those grey, lonely hours and the passing of days?

I would play it back,
I would never let it go.
My childhood is my safeguard, my best friend, my home.

If yesterday was a record,
Would you play it again?
I would.
I would put yesterday on repeat.

Edie Kelly (11)
Sydenham School, Sydenham

SMALL AND FRIGHTENED

Truth

Small and frightened,
They run,
Like small ants,
Nobody notices.

Small and frightened,
They trip,
The grip is strong but
They run on.

Small and frightened,
They hide,
There's no ride home,
They're trapped till the end.

They're small and frightened,
Do you know how that feels?
If you do, please share your news,
Then maybe I'll share mine.

Small and frightened!

Ashley Lefante (12)
Sydenham School, Sydenham

STRONG

Dare

I am strong.
So why am I classified with pink?
Pink.
Like frills,
Dresses,
Skirts
And sparkles.

He is weak.
So why is he classified with blue?
Blue.
Like metal,
Jeans,
Sea
And bruises.

Together we are strong.
So why can't we be seen that way?
Why can't we be seen as purple?
All together.
Seen one way.
Just open your eyes and look.
We are together.
We are strong.

Anna Williams (11)
Sydenham School, Sydenham

UNDER THE KNIFE

Truth

Some time in my life,
I'll go under the knife,
Once I hit puberty
(A year after that).

Scoliosis is the worst,
I've had it since birth
And I have to wear
A big, heavy back brace.

I have a funny-shaped spine,
So then they'll cut in a line,
On my back, on a bed,
In a hospital GOSH.

Some time in my life,
I'll go under the knife,
Once I hit puberty
(A year after that).

Greta Kelly (11)
Sydenham School, Sydenham

BOMBS ON FRIDAY

Dare

The wings have been built,
So have the dead.
They flew through the sky,
The moment it has been said.
The girl says no,
But they won't listen.
The birds let go,
One after one.
Scream and shout, fall in pain,
She's crying for help.

Heads on their heads digging straight down,
We think we are safe down in these holes.
Maybe we are,
Maybe we are not.

But she is still sad,
She is still hurt.

Layla Molina-Tittle (11)
Sydenham School, Sydenham

SUMMER

Truth

It's that thing that everyone seems to like
A time where you can just sit back and relax
Go on holiday, leave all your struggles behind
The sun, the sand and the sea
All the ice cream you eat
You never want to leave this paradise
All the memories you made
That face of disappointment when you get on that plane
The long, boring journey back home
You're there looking out at the grey, misty sky
Wishing you were still there
Summer.

Edith Sargeant (11)
Sydenham School, Sydenham

WOMEN'S RIGHTS

Dare

Suffragettes fought for women's rights,
They fought day and night,
But they were very right,
To fight for women's rights.

They punched a policeman in the face,
To get into the big place.
They went on strike,
To fight for women's rights.

They chained themselves to parliament,
They showed their commitment.
One got inside and locked herself in a cupboard overnight,
To fight for women's rights.

Poppie Lola Sweetman (11)
Sydenham School, Sydenham

STEREOTYPES

Dare

Stereotypes make people feel like they have to change,
The truth is nobody has to feel that way.
Girls like pink, boys like blue,
Nonsense, all of it nonsense,
So stop the stereotypes.

Stereotypes, stereotypes, make people feel sad,
Stereotypes, stereotypes, make people feel bad.
Stereotypes, stereotypes, they say girls like pink
And boys like blue.
Stereotypes, stereotypes, they are not true,
So stop the stereotypes.

Isla Steven (11)
Sydenham School, Sydenham

BIG JOURNEY

Truth

Waiting and waiting, it took forever,
Until before we knew it, it was September.
She packed and packed until all was done,
Then we had a long chat in the sun.

We got in the car, ate, slept and ate,
I couldn't believe we got there so late.
Unpacking took forever and ever,
The rain had stopped, so bring on sunny weather.

We left my sister all grown up,
Which left me to think, what will I do when I grow up?

Saffron Salsone (11)
Sydenham School, Sydenham

SCHOOL

Truth

I was the oldest in the school
Now I am the youngest.
The first day of school, *boom!*
Everyone was towering over me
I'm like a little mouse in a herd of elephants.
I took a step and walked to my class
Click-clack, when the pip goes off
It's clapping in my ears.
I love this school with all my heart
It's easy to make friends
All the teachers are super-duper kind.
I never want to leave.

Brooke Miller (12)
Sydenham School, Sydenham

HOMELESS

Dare

Morning to night
They fight for the right
Summer to winter
They shiver and whimper

People don't notice
There is another world out there
Cold and tired
Told to be quiet

It's rough and tough
People stare and glare
Charities try their best
To find a home, please help

Morning to night
They fight for the right
Summer to winter
They shiver and whimper.

Callie Boydell-Loftus (11)
Sydenham School, Sydenham

THE STABLES IN THE WINTER

Truth

Horses' hooves crunching
A white blanket of snow covers the fields
Horses galloping at detailed snowflakes
Snow like cotton wool.

I get butterflies in my stomach
Every time I see the beautiful landscape
Of horses in the snow.

Who couldn't love horses in winter?
Because I sure do
I love horses in winter
They make me feel all warm and fuzzy inside
Even when it's cold outside.

Poppy Mona Frayne-Cradick (12)
Sydenham School, Sydenham

MY FAVOURITE THINGS

Truth

I love dancing and prancing in the rain
And catching butterflies as a game
Colouring pencils one by one
An hour later and it's all done!
Reading is fun but until months later,
It's still not done.

I ate and ate until there was no ice cream
The reason for this
Was because the sun was beaming
And my heart was beating for ice cream.
I also like to jump until I go *kerplunk!*

Theodora Carneiro E Silva (11)
Sydenham School, Sydenham

MOON AND STARS

Dare

We watch the moon and stars,
Yearning a speck of dust,
Only to see something that's too far,
We feel it is a must.
To see how the planets' aligning affects us,
We send rockets up into outer space,
To see what we need to adjust,
To save the human race.
There are nine planets orbiting the sun,
Yet we only live on one,
Earth is ready to be done,
But are we ready to have a population of none?

Raphaelle Aklama (12)
Sydenham School, Sydenham

THE TRUE EARTH

Truth

Did they mean to do this?
What's the world coming to?
Was this supposed to happen?
What do we do?
Only God knows,
The magnificent world is spinning too slow.

People just care about money and fame,
And why don't they just take the blame?
Earth screams for help but no one listens,
When the world comes to an end, they'll all see,
But no one cares that it will be too late.

Shathana Satkunaseelan (11)
Sydenham School, Sydenham

INSANE

Dare

WWI had lots of deaths
Happily, in Heaven, they lay and rest
All the soldiers fought their best
They all thought of what the future would be like
They all fought for our country
Reading about WWI was not at all fun
Knowing how the soldiers felt
Made my heart melt
All the agony and pain
Made my tears fall like rain
The great World War was insane,
Insane! Insane! Insane!

Torree Henry (11)
Sydenham School, Sydenham

THE RIBBON

Truth

The ribbon of peace
The ribbon of war,
A ribbon apiece
Or to tie up some cords.
A lost ribbon of a pointe shoe
A ribbon that gave the chief a clue,
A ribbon from a golden jubilee,
A ribbon from a wife screaming with glee.
A ribbon in a book that reminds you where to look,
A ribbon to reward, the bravest of them all,
A ribbon of a world that existed no more.

Allegra McAuliffe (11)
Sydenham School, Sydenham

QUESTION

Truth

If I say yes,
But you say no,
Who is right?
If I say maybe
And you say affirmative,
Who is wrong?
If I say I agree,
But you say you disagree,
Who do people believe?
How do we know who's right and who's wrong?
Because if I say yes
And you say no,
All I wonder is,
Who is right and who is wrong?

Josie Gerard Hughes (11)
Sydenham School, Sydenham

MY FAVOURITE ANIMAL IS A WOLF

Truth

My favourite animal is a wolf,
It prowls and growls all night long.
Fine fur keeps them warm,
My favourite animal is a wolf.
Their claws are as sharp as knives
And their eyes are as green as emeralds.
My favourite animal is a wolf.
They are nocturnal animals,
All white, grey and sleek.
My favourite animal is a wolf.

Vivien Uong (11)
Sydenham School, Sydenham

UNTITLED

Truth

The first day that I got my dog
I was filled with joy.
My fingers could not wait to touch
The adorable brown, fluffy animal.
After five years I saw her lying on the floor in pain,
There was more water in my eyes than the ocean.
I search through my memories in my heart of my dog
And collect each one with joy.

Sydney Austin (11)
Sydenham School, Sydenham

WE'RE HERE FOR YOU!

Truth

We don't bully
Everyone is kind
Whatever you look like
We don't mind.

Words do hurt
I don't know why
But all I know is
It always makes me cry.

Bullies are not cool
You guys are just cruel
We all have got to stay strong
Because the bullies are always wrong.

Tiana Christina Williams (11)
Sydenham School, Sydenham

THE WAR WAS HARD

Dare

I watched the soldiers flood in,
A sea of khaki green,
Needing immediate help.
The tears that trickled down my face,
I remember very well.

Not knowing if he was going to die
Or stay alive,
Blood poured out of him like a tap.
The war was hard!
The war was extremely hard!

Grace Howlett (11)
Sydenham School, Sydenham

MY BEST FRIEND

Dare

My best friend is super,
My best friend is cool,
My best friend rules!
My best friend is unique.
Her name is Kesia.

K ind Kesia is always here
E xcept on Saturdays
S illy Kesia makes me laugh
I ncredible and fine
A mazing in her own style!

Rihanna Harvey (11)
Sydenham School, Sydenham

BULLIES

Truth

B ullying hurts
U nderstand their feelings
L onely and sad
L et's make a change
Y ou should have power over your own actions.

Rukhiaya Mahmood (12)
Sydenham School, Sydenham

THE DARK TRUTH

Truth

Trapped in this cage,
With a million others.
Begging, pleading, dying
In front of the Asian Hitler.

Letting us get slayed,
One by one.
Telling his people that we were heroes of the country,
But... are pawns momentous really?

A hundred agonies seen from day to night,
I just can't get all that torment to be out of sight.
Don't worry friends, I'll avenge your death someday,
The raves were heard by none but a small bird.

The screaming, the crying,
The nightmare is still ongoing.
There's no more hope for us,
I wish there was a chance for freedom.

Unable to see the future,
Unable to escape the horrendous devil.
But I still believe in freedom,
And freedom is what the world needs.

Jacky Li (14)
Thomas Tallis School, Blackheath

FREEDOM

Dare

Everyday life is gay,
Every day we happily live and play,
Every day we have our own lives,
In this world, freedom and fun thrives.

We are not blind, we can all see
That this is as true as can be,
It's as simple as a cup of tea:
We all know the world is free.

We can do what want, so long as it's within the law,
Though sometimes we're restricted from things, we don't know what for.
How should I know better? The past I've forgot,
I think we're all free, maybe not?

But it must be true, it's all they tell us,
On a train or on a bus.
Every day; into our minds it's rammed,
Though some freedoms are still banned.

Why are we told nothing but lies?
Why, no longer, are there blue skies?

How can I tell you what's right or wrong,
If there's no such thing allowed as a poem or song?

Every day, we know they're not right.
Every day we resist to fight.
Every day, more hope is lost.
Every day, there's only happiness for a cost.

There's nothing stopping us
From calling out with glee;
Because we are all free,
aren't we?

Freddie J H C Fullerton (13)
Thomas Tallis School, Blackheath

TRUTH

Truth

Sometimes I feel I am in a labyrinth of lies,
Every twist and turn leading to a demon of cries.
The Minotaur waits for a slip-up, a mistake
Leaving precious friendships trailing in its wake.

They roll off your tongue like a rhythm, a flow,
Waiting for someone to figure out the code.
It's sweet for a moment then the second turns sour
When you realise your words are now out of your power.

Be yourself, be kind, be truthful, be free,
Not trapped by your lies in a dark room with no key.

Susie Duckworth (11)
Thomas Tallis School, Blackheath

FREE

Dare

Free, free
That's what I want to be
Not being trapped and hidden
Away from the world.

Free, free
Something I hope
To be one day.

Free, free
Is not what I am
Unfortunately.

Free, free
Can you imagine being in my shoes?
Free, free
Something I dearly wish to be!

Lily Ijoma (12)
Thomas Tallis School, Blackheath

LIGHT AND DARK

Dare

Deep in the darkness of death,
I am the glimmering light.
I will grow as the years pass
Even if I am the only one to fight.

If they knock me down
I'll always get back up.
I am my master.
I make my own fate.

Lewis Atkins (13)
Thomas Tallis School, Blackheath

YOUNG WRITERS INFORMATION

We hope you have enjoyed reading this book – and that you will continue to in the coming years.

If you're a young writer who enjoys reading and creative writing, or the parent of an enthusiastic poet or story writer, do visit our website **www.youngwriters.co.uk**. Here you will find free competitions, workshops and games, as well as recommended reads, a poetry glossary and our blog.

If you would like to order further copies of this book, or any of our other titles, then please give us a call or visit **www.youngwriters.co.uk**.

Young Writers
Remus House
Coltsfoot Drive
Peterborough
PE2 9BF
(01733) 890066
info@youngwriters.co.uk